STEPPING INTO COURAGE

By Tricia Andreassen

Co-Authored by:
Kate Bancroft
Chris Blackburn
Tom Cain
Janet DiTroia
Dave Frett
Lydia Gates
Chris McClure
Garrett Milby
Edward Reed
Karen White
Terry Wood

Creative Life
Publishing & Learning
INSTITUTE

Creative Life Publishing & Learning Institute
www.CLPLI.com
Info@CLPLI.com

Book Versions
Paperback ISBN: 978-1-946265-07-4
eBook ISBN: 978-1-946265-08-1
Amazon ISBN: 978-1-946265-09-8

Cover Design By Dara Rogers

CONTENTS

Introduction | 1

The Day of April 17 | 5
by Tricia Andreassen

Me, Myself And Chocolate | 19
by Kate Bancroft

What You Will Not Face, You Cannot Overcome | 31
by Chris Blackburn

A Changed Life | 43
by Tom Cain

Leave The Light On… | 51
by Janet DiTroia

The Great Exchange of Lost and Found | 61
by Dave Frett

Freedom From Fear In Courage To Forgive | 73
by Lydia Gates

Keep In Step With The Spirit | 81
by Chris McClure

Do The Thing Which You Think You Cannot Do | 93
by Garrett Milby

The Making Of A Warrior | 105
by Edward Reed

Lynda's Lessons | 119
by Karen White

Overcome Fear by Exercising Courage | 131
by Terry Wood

INTRODUCTION

I remember one winter day driving back to my home in North Carolina after being in Georgia for a while writing and working in solitude. I had led a group of *authors* on a book project that I had already mapped out, but on the way home my heart began to stir within me. I started to think about those times when long seasons of change, uncertainty and struggle come and the results that come with them.

I thought back to a friend of mine who had gone through a difficult divorce, had two boys in high school, and was struggling both financially and emotionally after being married for 25 years. At one point, she said it was hard to feel hopeful when things seemed to stack up at every turn and it felt like no headway could be made.

As I thought of conversations with women and men about walking through their daily lives, there were varying degrees of the obstacles they faced—but one thing seemed to be the constant.

Hope is so greatly needed in our lives (and yes, there is a book on HOPE in progress). But, what became clear to me, in prayer and talking to myself out loud, was something happens in our core where we lose all hope and we are unable to feel like good even exists around the corner. I began to process this reality and called my cousin Elizabeth who is also a writer to talk it out. It became clear to me that, when hope is lost, it is because we have succumbed to fear and allowed it to grow and manifest like thick weeds within our soul choking every breath from us that we need for hope to grow again.

After finishing the call with Elizabeth, I still had several hours of drive time, so I continued to process: *"Okay Tricia, so if fear takes over to such levels that hope is lost, how do we go about battling fear because that is the core issue?"* In my continued internal conversation, I recognized that when I have been stuck and hesitant on making a decision, often times I didn't want to admit I was afraid. You see, I didn't want to CALL IT FEAR. I would use other words instead—for example:

"I'm hesitant"

"I'm uncomfortable"

"I'm not sure"

Even recently while talking to one of my close friends Mark, I started to say, *"I'm afraid that…"* and (almost as soon as the words escaped my mouth) I said: *"Well, I don't want to say afraid. I meant…"*

He said, *"That's ok, you can say it."* So I continued on.

In this realization and in the research I do on human mindset and behavior, I continue to gain broader knowledge and deeper understanding on these subjects that I know I will never completely understand even if I live another hundred years. The interfusion of how our spirit, mind and body work (in relation to our life experiences and beliefs created from those experiences) is incredibly complicated like the decoding of the DNA within the cell.

This is why I push within my own spirit to ask questions that are often difficult to answer. *"If fear grabs us to a point that can make us run or make us freeze, and basically cuts us off at the knees from possible breakthrough to something that could be potentially wonderfully life changing, how do we battle that? What is the one thing that we can use to fight fear?"*

At that moment, my mind began to meld with my heart. I sincerely knew God was at work in me and the crystal clear answer that came to me was *'COURAGE'*.

Driving in that car that day, I felt the exhilaration and rush of adrenaline. Yes! That was it! What was Fear's biggest enemy? Courage! When we find courage, even if it is just a little courage but act on it, in that moment the monster of fear begins to shrink and become exposed for what it truly is.

That is the purpose of this book. My hope is that all of us (who are sharing our stories and teachings with you) can help you fight fear and find courage because, you see my friend, it is in courage that the beautiful existence of the incredible warrior within each of us... emerges!

THE DAY OF APRIL 17

By Tricia Andreassen

THE DAY OF APRIL 17

I stayed at my mom's house the night before last, because we were in the process of packing to move into our new house. I could discount these experiences I had today from the things I saw and experienced at my mom's home, but I feel that just connecting it all to the flow of my mind would be discounting how God works through us.

I must have slept soundly because I woke up at 4:29 AM feeling relatively awake. I don't recall any dreams through the night while I was sleeping. I took my journal and Bible, and sat on my mom's sofa. Sincerely, I don't think I sat there for longer than 30 minutes and my eyes felt heavy. At my mom's house, she doesn't have an easy way to make coffee. Her normal morning activity is to go to McDonald's to have breakfast and visit with her friends, so the only coffee easily accessible was instant decaf which probably explains why I felt the urge to go back to sleep.

In those two short hours of sleep, I ended up having a dream. The night before I had been praying, seeking God and asking to feel the presence of the Holy Spirit. I wanted to feel Him like I had in the past. It wasn't like I hadn't felt Him in a while. It was more that I was just craving the feeling of His Spirit with me.

The Dream

I had a dream where I wanted to see *"these cats at a home where they were being given away"*. They were not little baby kittens, but relatively young and they were brother and sister. My son Jordan went with me to see them. I didn't know whether or not my husband Kurt would approve of my taking both of them, but while I was there I ended up meeting two little boys (one 6 and one 9 and a half) who were in foster care with this couple. I am not sure what happened to their parents, but it was somehow spiritually-implied that they needed parent figures in their lives. The home they lived in was a temporary arrangement—these boys needed more than that.

As I visited there, my heart started to call to me about bringing these two boys into our home. These boys were so loving, but I especially connected with the 6 year old. When I left and got back to Kurt, I mentioned my experiences. He reluctantly agreed to go with me to their home. I am not sure whether we were going for the cats or for the kids. It was like *"both"*. I felt we could resolve the situation.

We left home but, on the way back over to the place where the boys and cats were waiting, I got a call about someone who was interested in our house. I answered that it was sold, and with disappointment the caller responded *"OK"*.

Kurt said he felt comfortable with us taking the 6 year old and the one young cat. I knew the young cat had an illness of some kind—I knew that she needed care. As we entered the house, we were also thinking through the process of what we would need to do to take the 6 year old with us. We were asking about things like *"what paperwork we needed to sign"* and *"were we taking him home with us that day"*.

The other little boy started to cry. He was there hearing what was going on and realized that he might be left behind. He so much wanted to live with us too. I asked him how old he was. He told me he was going to be 10 in a few months. Even though my heart was calling, I knew Kurt wasn't comfortable with taking both of them and in some way I knew that I understood his whys. While hugging the older boy, I whispered into his ear that I would see what I could do for him to come live with us or at least to stay close to his brother. I had a knowing in my spirit that they had been abandoned, with no mother or father in their life. I knew they needed this.

It was hard to leave the older little boy because I knew he needed a loving home, but I also felt like, while it was at a time when things weren't settled for us, he was going to be reunited with his brother and receive good care. I had a hope or a knowing that things were going to work out with all of this.

In my right arm, I was holding something like a baby that was being cuddled, but logically I knew in my dream it was not the 6 year old because he was much bigger than that. Was it possibly the cat I was holding in the same way I used to hold my cat bundled like a baby to love on it? It was not clear to me.

Toward the end of the dream, the perspective changes from first person to third person almost like another story. I am shown there is a grieving man who had just lost his wife who had died. There was a foreshadowing that he would find his way to the older boy and adopt him, giving him a new home.

In this foreshadowing, I became an observer who saw the story unfold like watching a movie. The woman who had the 9 year old was going to be alone too with no husband. But, it was a part of the process of life and these two were going to find each other, and soon the brothers would be together again.

I began to feel like this dream was a story or a movie of some kind about the woman whose husband had died. She had rescued the one baby kitten and the little 6 year old boy, but now she was going to meet the man who had adopted the old brother and now they were going to be a family as one.

It was a sad yet happy ending at the same time—representing love and loss all in one story, as well as new the boys reuniting for healing and closure.

I woke from this dream with a feeling I had to write it down because it was a message that could be a book or a movie. So I went to the living room right away to write it down before I forgot it. I was able to get the basics down of the dream and I proceeded to get ready for the day.

Before heading to Wildacres Retreat (I call it: Going to The Mountain), I needed to stop by my home and pick up a few things. While at the house, I gathered some last odds and ends—like my coffee pot which I wanted to take with me. I got back in the car and tried to call my friend Mark, but he didn't answer. My little voice told me to give a call to Kate Bancroft, who I don't call too much because we talk by text and online more often. But, that morning, something in my heart called to me to talk with her about us working together for women doing retreats and conferences.

In less than a minute, I drove by a woman on the side of the road bending over petting this cat that appeared to have been struck by a car. I told Kate that I saw this and needed to call her back. I just had to see if the woman needed help to take the cat to the vet or something.

I turned around on Webbs Road. By the time I got to the place where the woman had been, she was no longer standing on the side of the road and I didn't see the cat. What I did see was a minivan in a gravel driveway, so I pulled in near it and walked toward the van. As I came around the corner, I saw this woman probably in her 60's cradling a cat like a baby. She was crying and the cat was not moving.

At that moment, I said: *"I am so so sorry. Is he dead?"* She nodded her head and said yes with tears on her cheeks. I stood there with her and reach around her to hug her. I don't know why, but the love I had for this woman and the cat was so strong. I looked at the woman and said, *"Is this your cat?"* She replied, *"Yes."* It was now being confirmed to me that she had found her beloved cat on the side of the road—gone.

Immediately I said to her, *"I have anointing oil in my car. Would it be okay if I got it?"* She said *"Yes."* She stayed there holding the cat, not moving from that back seat in her minivan. In the other back seat beside her was a child's car seat.

I returned with the anointing oil and anointed both the women and the cat and prayed over them. I asked God to comfort this woman and to bless the soul of this sweet cat (as I knew that God had a special place in heaven for the animals that he created for this earth). I can't explain it but I understood God's love for all living things, not just man but for the hearts of all creatures.

After prayer, I stayed with her and I shared how I had just had a dream the night before of two cats (a brother and a sister in need of a home) and how I wasn't sure but perhaps in her loss God was going to bless her when she was ready to receive a new cat into her life. She shared that this cat, whose name was Kat, had been a stray she had taken in to love; it was basically an unofficial adoption because she had put up signs to find the owner and no one had claimed her.

The Realization

After I left this woman, I had an overwhelming realization that the woman was cuddling her cat the EXACT same way I had been shown in my dream just a few hours before. I picked the phone back up to call Kate. While on the phone, the confirmation overtook me with such a *"knowing"* that I began to cry because God had given me this dream to show me so much. Even as I share this right now, I understand that we all need love and we all need a place that we can feel home where we feel like we are a part of something. We want to be loved in a family and we want to GIVE love. Yet in loss, grief, and even feeling alone or lost, we sometimes feel like we have been abandoned.

After getting off the phone with Kate, I returned Mark's call and we talked about what had just transpired. I couldn't fully explain the feeling the Lord had given me. I was already in a spirit of contemplation on this day after Easter, thinking about how Christ did so much work AFTER his death to bring such profound healing and change.

My heart was filled with just a fraction of what Christ really feels for us and, in that fraction of *"feeling"*, my love was so pure and compassionate. It was a taste of how much He loves us and all that we have here. His love for all living things as He mentioned in the Sermon on the Mount—just the thought of His knowing everything, appreciation of the sparrow, the flowers, the children, and all nature … was overwhelming me with a vision in my mind of a circle of people together. It is so hard to describe the expectancy I felt of what God would be doing this week and over the next three weeks, specifically in the work He has been training me to do.

The next divine encounter

I was still on my headset talking with Mark when I pulled in the real estate office to drop off our earnest money check for our new home. As I was walking in to the office, a senior age couple was coming out of the office. As the spirit of the Lord was on me I said joyously, *"So did you just list your home for sale!?"* They said, *"We sure did! Here is the paperwork!"* I didn't know them at all but, while in the spirit of the Lord, I didn't even second guess what came out of my mouth. I said, *"Could I pray for your move to be smooth and for your home to sell?"* They joyously said, *"Yes!"*

Right there in the parking lot, I gathered the three of us together in a circle and I began to pray over this lovely couple whom I had never met before this moment. When we were done, we all rejoiced and hugged in that circle gathering—right there in the parking lot. The woman then asked me *"Do you have a church in this area?"* I shared that I was a part of Elevation Church in Charlotte, but Elevation had started a branch here, and I was looking forward to being a part of it. I shared that I did ministry work too, but didn't go into detail because the conversation was God appointed. Within moments, she looked at me and said, *"Would you please pray over something for me?"* *"Absolutely"* I replied, not knowing what it was.

She had such courage in that moment sharing with me, a total stranger until just moments before, about the pain that was in their family relationships. Before she even spoke the words, I knew this woman needed prayer for strength and yet, as a mother loves her child with such unconditional love, she asked me to please pray for her daughter.

Years ago, her daughter and son-in-law were expecting a baby and found out that the baby was going to be on a vent to live. To save the child, the family had to make a decision whether to have the vent on or off which caused great sadness because the baby didn't live. The daughter had gotten pregnant again and the same scenario happened which created a deeper crevice of pain to the level that both of sets of parents became estranged in their relationship. Each of them, the parents and the grandparents, had experienced so much loss and in that process had both been so misunderstood that the relationship crumbled.

"That is why we are selling our house" she confided. Their daughter

had decided to move away and hadn't even told them. It was like another death to this lovely couple in their 70's. The husband held his wife beside him, sharing his grief as well. They also shared that they had raised their other grandson born to their son for all of his life. At the age of 19, he was killed in a car accident. He had been the light in their darkness to overcome the grief of the relationship between the daughter and her parents. When he was killed, they were devastated. The man shared, *"Not a day goes by that we don't think of him."* She chimed in saying that she did crafting over the years and when her grandson was just two years old he would help her sew. He loved her crafting and the blankets she would make.

In sharing that story of her daughter and the loss of her grandson she revealed to me, *"Tricia, on the way over here to sign the listing, I realized that, since Chance (her grandson) has been gone, I have been hoarding all these craft materials because Chance always loved the work I did."*

At that moment I said, *"Wow! You do crafts! Crafts are a part of my ministry work with women. I help them do art projects while they are working through things. I teach them how to unlock their feelings in journaling. The art is a way of therapy in the healing process. In fact, that is where I am heading now—to do some writing and retreat scheduling for doing this work with women in their healing process with writing and art."*

I don't think I will ever forget the look on her face while we were still standing there in that real estate parking lot. She looked at me and said, *"Do you have somewhere you need to be? Are you on a deadline to be somewhere?"* I replied, *"No, not really. I am on my way up to the mountain to my retreat."* I didn't know why she was asking, but I just let it flow. She had such a look of love and said, *"I would love you to come to my home. I want to give you some of my art supplies because you can help others."*

In that moment, my heart was so full. At the same time, between what happened just an hour or so earlier with the woman and the cat, I can say that I was in an amazed state. What God was doing in showing me the confirmation of the conversation I had with my friend Kate and revealing how our hearts process our feelings, I don't even know how I can fully put words to this experience.

The couple gave me their phone number and their address, so I could come over after they ran some errands. Within that hour, I was at their home and she welcomed me in with such a sweet love. She guided me to a bedroom that had been converted to a sewing and craft room where there were organized supplies of yarn, felt, quilt pieces, as well as rolls upon rolls of beautiful lace. She began to fill up a large box with these things. Then she opened another drawer for crafting jewelry and began to load from that one too. By the time we were finished, my trunk was overflowing with items to work with women and with youth. It was at least several hundred dollars of materials that she openly gave to me.

Before leaving, we stood in their master bedroom (I went in to check to see if I could help them with something on the computer) just visiting with one another. She went into her drawer and brought over to me a brochure of her grandson's memorial. It was a picture of this beautiful young man and a poem that he had written as a youth about his love for God and the work on this earth we are to do.

They shared stories about how loving he was and how he openly gave hugs to elderly widowed women in the church and his mission work to help kids in downtown Philadelphia. They were so incredibly proud of their grandson. Holding that paper showing his picture and the legacy of words that lived on beyond his life here, I asked them if I could share his poem in my next book. They said they would be honored because it would give Chance's life and legacy an opportunity to continue on.

They walked me to my car and we hugged. They invited me back again after I would get back from my travels, telling me she had more crafts for me to give. What was so interesting was they said to me, *"You have been such a blessing to us today."* And to that comment I replied, *"YOU have been the blessing to me."*

Even writing this now, the tears stream down my face realizing how God worked through all three of us. I didn't even realize until this moment that this would be my chapter in this book on Courage. However in the process of writing this, I see the framework of Courage in action.

It takes courage to show our real hearts openly.

It takes courage to love when there is such a risk of loss and hurt.

It takes courage to be ourselves with the possibility that, when we show our authentic self, we may be rejected, misunderstood, or not accepted.

It takes courage to allow God to work through us and to release the uncertainty of where He may lead us in life.

So why fight the fear and have the courage to love again, why fight the fear to share deeply and expose our pain?

Because in the process of stepping into courage and moving forward, there are the most priceless gifts, more precious than anything we can imagine in this world. This story I share covered a span of just ONE DAY...ONE DAY.

Love took over.

Fear stepped aside.

Faith showed up.

Courage was revealed.

ABOUT TRICIA ANDREASSEN

Tricia Andreassen has a mission—a *"life calling"* she describes like this:

"My mission is to bring teaching and strategies to breakthrough challenges struggles, and obstacles that show up daily in our business and personal lives. Each person has a purpose and calling. I want to help as many people as possible discover what God has placed in their heart to do."

As a young entrepreneur, Tricia bought her first real estate investment property at age 19 and has been active in the real estate industry since then. Early on, she began to see principles and strategies that could be applied to help companies of all types build their brand, message and organization.

Andreassen started her company in grass roots fashion from the bonus room of her house with her toddler son literally on her hip and grew it into one of the most internationally recognizable companies within the target market it services. After almost 15 years as CEO, she sold her company to pursue her passion by expanding her personal coaching practice in business advancement into the fields of spiritual development and personal growth.

As her mission progresses, Tricia's growing life story continues to be told with a central message of persistence, resilience and faith woven into insightful strategies that heals the soul and transform results. Her passion is to creatively deliver, inspire, motivate and strategize lasting change through writing, speaking, teaching, the arts (including songwriting) in intimate gatherings such as workshops and retreats that focus on unlocking inner warrior strength.

For more than 25 years, Tricia has helped thousands of people with their lives and businesses. One of her companies, Creative Life Publishing and Learning Institute, was founded with the mission to help writers become authors and to bring teaching and training programs centered on faith, leadership, youth, parenting, business building, marketing and spiritual growth. Her business book Interfusion Marketing hit #1 in less than 5 hours and remained on the best-seller list for 59 weeks.

John Maxwell, the world's #1 ranked leadership expert, has certified team member Andreassen as both Speaker and Coach to teach leadership, personal growth and youth development programs. Her credentials also include an Executive Coach ACTP certification through the International Coaching Federation that positions Tricia to bring uniquely creative strategies to organizations, schools, ministry groups and leaders from all walks of life. She has three published books, an additional five more books in process, and an international radio show called Unlock Your Inner Warrior with Tricia Andreassen.

Contact Tricia:
- Website: www.MsUnstoppable.com
- LinkedIn: www.LinkedIn.com/in/TriciaAndreassen
- Facebook: www.Facebook.com/BeUnstoppableNow
- YouTube: www.UnstoppableWarriorWithin.net
- Twitter: www.Twitter.com/TriciaSings
- Instagram: www.Instagram.com/BeUnstoppableNow
- Radio Show: www.UnlockYourInnerWarrior.com

ME, MYSELF AND CHOCOLATE

By Kate Bancroft

ME, MYSELF AND CHOCOLATE

Chocoholic: a person who is addicted to or excessively fond of chocolate

Driving home from work, the sky was black from the storm. Tears were pouring from my eyes as fast as the rain hitting the windshield. I was a mess, pure misery. Hives, the size of my fingers, had once again taken over.

My doctor had no answer for me. I was sent to a dermatologist who only treats what he can see and of course when I was there, there were no hives! Having no clue as to what is causing them, how can I make an appointment that takes place when I am having issues (hint: that is why I went to the doctor)?

My mom suggested keeping a food journal to determine if there was a connection to this cycle of hives. Both my mom and her sister had problems with chocolate which gave them headaches. Headaches and hives are not the same thing! Desperate for relief, willing to try anything, I began. Quickly, the culprit became obvious. This had to be a mistake! Something so dear to me could never be the problem. I couldn't be expected to live without it.

On the way home, having had an exceptionally rough day, I stopped to get something to take the edge off. After all, I needed it with the day I had. My answer to my problem was, of course, chocolate. Every woman knows that chocolate solves everything! I was not yet finished with my chocolate when my new friend Hives arrived to torture me. The nightmare was true—chocolate was behind this sinister plot of misery. *"Just stop eating it"* said my husband. What does he know? He cannot possibly understand! He has never had PMS! I'm a *"give me your chocolate and no one gets hurt"* kind of woman.

I struggled for months knowing it was chocolate that was causing the hives. I said I wouldn't eat it,but couldn't seem to stop. I would lie about eating it, hide it, sneak off to have some. Who was I trying to fool? Hello! Hives everywhere! The only 12 step program for chocolate lovers is to never be more than 12 steps away from it.

The day came when I just couldn't take anymore. Sitting in my car with a candy bar, covered in hives, face drenched with tears, I was feeling hopeless. I had reached the end of myself. I cried out to God, I wanted to stop but I couldn't do it. I wasn't strong enough.

I heard a voice in my head that was so clear and so peaceful say *"But I can."* It was like a life line to a drowning person. I was so new in my faith in God that I didn't even know I could ask Him for help. When I heard that I could, I did something that I didn't know you really shouldn't do—I said *"Okay God, go for it and this is how it needs to be done!"* In His mercy, He covered me in grace and I have been a recovering *"chocoholic"* for over 20 years.

My *"love affair"* with food began years earlier. I was playing summer league softball. I had missed a ball at home plate and had to run after it. I heard a woman in the stands laugh and say *"That's okay, she needs the exercise! She's rather chubby!"*. When I got home, I weighed myself, choose a number that sounded the opposite of chubby and stopped eating. I was in total control of everything that went into my mouth until my parents realized something was wrong and demanded that I eat (at the cost of all I held dear had I refused). I perfected the art of eating in front of them then removing everything I had just eaten. This crazy cycle went on for years. Just to make my life more interesting, binge eating joined the party. I was one talented, multi-faceted, mixed-up eating disorder diva.

So what does this have to do with fear? In my journey to find freedom from eating disorders, I can tell you, for me, it has everything to do with fear: fear of not fitting in, fear of not being good enough, fear of being laughed at, and all pieces of the fear of rejection.

Growing up, I had a speech problem. I was quite difficult to understand and was picked on a lot. In the third grade, we had to tell the class what we would remember most about the person sitting next to us if they were to die tomorrow. I know: great assignment for an 8 year old. The girl I was seated next to told the class that the only thing she would remember about me was the funny way I talk. Everyone laughed. Even the teacher chuckled, before she caught herself. I just wanted to disappear.

That was the final straw for me. I decided that I would stop talking in school, that I would never allow myself to be put in the position to be laughed at, and that I would become invisible. This is how I would survive. Keep my head down and don't make eye contact. The woman at the softball game had no idea what her chuckle and her words did to me.

Can you hear that hurt little girl who made those decisions? She stood up behind the big, thick walls she built and screamed *"Not going there again! Not happening! Not on my watch!"* She went into full blown protection mode. Did I know why I reacted as I did? Now I do, but then, all I could do was react out of my fear.

My fear of people laughing at me was the heart of my response. It wasn't my fear of being fat. Before that day being fat had never crossed my mind. So, thanks for that new one! It was that fear of rejection that fueled my eating disorders. Food never rejects you, never hurts your feelings, never makes you feel unworthy and never laughs at you. I can eat when I want, what I want, and how I want. I am in control. If I have control, then I am safe.

In the book of Exodus, God calls Moses to free the Israelites from Egypt. Moses has a long list of reasons why he can't go. *"I'm slow of speech. They won't listen to me. Who am I to go?"* He is full of *"supposes and what if's"*. Can you hear it—the fear of rejection, failure, and not being good enough? Going back to Egypt brings up the reasons he had left which he had not resolved. He had been comfortably living in Midian these past 40 years. We mistake comfort for safety from our fear. In truth, it keeps us stuck in our fear.

Moses did return to Egypt. God enlisted Aaron to help Moses move forward. As Moses followed God's direction, with every act of obedience, his confidence became stronger and his fears became smaller. Courage isn't the absence of fear. It is action you take while you are afraid.

As John Wayne said: *"Courage is being scared to death but saddling up anyway."*

In Exodus 14, the Israelites are freed from slavery. Moses is leading them to the promise land. Panic hits the camp when they realize the Egyptians were after them. Fear spreads and they cry out that it would have been better to serve the Egyptians then to be free. The joy of God delivering them is pushed aside. They are on the way to the Promise land and fear has them wanting to quit and run for cover. All they can see is the Red Sea before them and the Egyptian army behind them. The situation looks hopeless. Moses goes before the Lord to seek guidance. God responds, *"Quit whining!"* (Kate paraphrase!) *"Tell the people to move forward."* Forward seems wrong, there is no way there. The only way out is to go back. They do move forward, Moses raises his staff and stretches out his hand as the Lord instructed. The Red Sea parts and they are saved.

Movement forward through our fear brings breakthrough from the fear.

We all have fear. We need to face our fear. Some of us hang out with it, give it a massage, decorate a room for it, and treat it like a pet.

In my high school, speech class was a requirement for graduation. I couldn't figure out why people were so upset. I thought it would be an easy class. After all, I spent 8 years in speech therapy. Imagine my first day in class when I discovered Speech class meant I had to get up in front of the entire class and talk.

My fear was all over me, consuming me as I begged (and begged) my parents to get me out of this class! I remember my dad saying *"Katie, if you want to graduate you are just going to have to figure it out."* Figure it out! What was there to figure out? Who cares if I graduate! I was not going to do it. There had to be a way out.

Our first assignment was a 3 minute speech. I was sick, scared, couldn't breathe, and sure I was going to die right there in front of the whole class. Keeping my eyes on the floor, I mumbled my way through about 30 seconds before I ran back to my seat crying. I put my head down on my desk and waited for the laughter. Only silence followed. With my head down, I watched the next person. With each speech, I sat up a little higher. I realized they were just as scared as I was. Not one person was comfortable up there. There were more than a few that looked like they were going to be sick. It was a great day as I realized I was not the only one in the *"scared to talk in front of people"* club.

The speech class opened a door to a world I didn't know existed. I didn't have to live in fear of talking to people. I had spent so long being ashamed of who I was and not wanting to be me that I didn't know anything about me. I began to gain the confidence to put myself in front of people.

Today, I speak in front large groups all over and enjoy every minute.

It is truly part of my DNA. In a group, unless they are booing and throwing things, it's easy to share my journey to freedom.

Philippians 4:13 *"I can do all things through Christ who gives me strength."*

2 Corinthians 12:9 *"My grace is sufficient for you, for My strength is made perfect in weakness."*

I am continuously amazed how God takes the source of great pain, shame and struggle and uses it for His glory. My parents had difficulty understanding me. Now God uses my voice to tell others of His goodness!

So, what are you afraid of? Fear can look like Mt Rushmore—overwhelming in size with 5 faces ready to tell you about your fears, doubts and worries to get you to give up. I want you to look at FEAR, really look at it. Ask yourself: Why does this make me afraid?

Asking questions about my fear helps me to gain clarity. This exercise helps me get to the root of my true fear. I would love to give credit to whom it's due for this exercise, but I am not sure where it came from.

I am going to use my softball story in the example to show you the questions in process:

What about the experience made me afraid?

I am afraid they think I am fat.

Okay, why is their thinking you are fat scary?

What if I don't fit in?

Okay, if you don't fit in, why is that scary?

What if they don't like me?

Okay, why is not being liked scary?

They might laugh at me.

Keep asking and move forward. Watch Mt. Rushmore shrink in size and the voices become quieter as you step over and through your fears.

So, what are you afraid of? How are you letting fear manage your life? For me, it comes back to food. We use food for so much for than what it's designed for. We eat when we are sad, happy, stressed, tired, lonely and the list goes on.

What, you thought chocolate was my only issue? Let's get real. Having only one would be too easy. I love sweets. If it's made of sugar, it's good! Perhaps you have heard of the condition called a *"Sweet Tooth"*? I have a mouth full of them! Sugar is the next best thing to chocolate! I know I am not the only one with this condition.

I didn't realize it was a problem until I went on a diet. This diet removed all sugar (gasp!) and flour. Do you know that you can be addicted to sugar and it's unpleasant coming off of that wonderful sugar rush? If you don't believe me, just ask my kids. My evil twin took my place for several days. The diet worked, I lost 20 pounds, and felt better than I think I had ever felt. I went back to my old eating habits. Hello caramel-covered, custard-filled Long John.

Happy days are here again! Six months later, I was back on the diet and the evil twin once again took up residence.

I heard someone say if you put *"it's just"* in front of something, it means you have a problem. *"It's just sugar. What's the problem?"* My problem was it was never enough. I am not the kind of person who can open a bag of cookies and only eat one. How do people do that?! How do you have Halloween candy left at Easter? I would have to throw my son's leftover candy away because he didn't eat it. Whose child is he?!

So I did what any spiritual person would do, I prayed and promised I would change. After all, I can't eat chocolate. A girl has got to have something!

Psalm 18:23b *"And I have kept myself from my iniquity. That which causes me to stumble I have to leave behind."*

Food—So much emotion is wrapped up around food.

If you are in the stranglehold of an eating disorder, you must seek professional help. There is freedom on the other side.

We make food such a big deal. I hear it so often, *"You can't have chocolate? I could never give that up. You have more willpower than I do"*. Actually, I am the weakest one I know. I believe God has me share this because I need to hear it! I am also gluten-free, sugar-free and allergic to several things. Now the question is *"What can you eat?"* So many people act as if life would be over for them, if they couldn't eat something. Oh, that's right, I did that! Is that you too?

Here are 2 verses that helped me walk out of the grip of sugar:

Psalm 18:37 *"I have pursued my enemies and overtaken them. Neither did I turn back again until they were destroyed."*

Joshua 1:9 *"Be strong and courageous."* Lean on His strength and get people around you who will support you.

Run away from anyone who says to you *"it's just one_____"*. Just one is taking you back before the starting line. Don't do it.

Do I miss bread? Yes! I was a huge bread fan. I choose not to eat it so I won't be sick for days. It's a mindset—It's not *"I can't"*. It's an *"I choose"* not to.

Look at what happened to Eve in the Garden. The enemy turned her focus onto the one thing she was not allowed to eat. She lost sight of everything she could enjoy and BAM! Here I am so many years later and I still don't fit in with the crowd. I no longer talk funny. Now, my food choices are *"funny"*.

On my journey with food, I discovered more freedom to be me. I learned how to walk through one thing at a time and stand in victory.

The struggle with chocolate laid the foundation for the path to discover what I truly fear and to recognize the reasons behind my emotions. My fear of rejection- yep it's still there. My mindset has changed. The 8 year old girl in me no longer calls the shots. The choice is all mine. I can step forward or I could pull an Eve and focus on what is a no-go.

I learned how to watch others enjoy what I no longer choose to eat without feeling like I am missing out. It is only food. I look at this from a temporary view point. After all, this isn't my true home. My life here is short compared to eternity. When I get to heaven, I will be free to eat anything that is there. I am certain it will be better than anything I could eat here.

I am asking Jesus if He would have my mother-in-law's sugar cookies and lemon bars waiting for me.

What, no chocolate?!

ABOUT KATE BANCROFT

Kate Bancroft understands how to turn weaknesses into strengths. Kate develops growth, brings hope and inspires women who are caught in the stranglehold of self-limiting belief, feeling unwanted, unworthy and the food they use to mask their pain. She is committed to walking with women on the journey to the breakthrough of these barriers so they can discover the treasure they are. Kate draws from her 30 plus years in ministry, customer service and her own life experiences to impact and transform lives through her coaching, writing and speaking. As the Director of Women's Ministry for Crossroads Community Church, Kate develops small group studies, creates events, trains ministry leaders and teaches discipleship classes.

Kate has certification through The John Maxwell Team as an Executive Leadership Coach, Personal Growth and Development Coach and Communications.

Kate is a recovering chocoholic and an eating disorder diva who lives down a little dirt road with the love of her life, her husband Brian.

Contact Kate:
- Website: www.JohnMaxwellGroup.com/KateBancroft
- LinkedIn: www.LinkedIn.com/in/Kate-Bancroft-967559104
- Facebook: www.Facebook.com/Kate.Bancroft.94
- Email: KateBancroftJMT@gmail.com

WHAT YOU WILL NOT FACE, YOU CANNOT OVERCOME

By Chris Blackburn

WHAT YOU WILL NOT FACE, YOU CANNOT OVERCOME

Casey Stengel, the famous manager of the New York Yankees in the 1950's, was quoted once in an interview that *"there comes a time in every man's life, and I've had plenty of them."* When it comes to fear, I don't think we have just one defining moment that we face, but many over the course of a lifetime that are meant to mold us, shape us and to help us grow into the man or woman God purposed us to be.

However, we all can look back on our lives and find that one moment that really sticks out in our memory. There is something about that one moment in time that seems to define us in a way that no other experience could. For me, the real moment I learned to deal with my fear came as a freshman in high school.

Before I get to that, I need to offer a little background. You see, when I was five years old, I almost died.

I remember that night, some forty years ago, as if it were yesterday. I had been having trouble breathing for months, but I would typically find a way to play through it. There were trips to Dr. Hall, Dr. Spillman and Dr. Cook, the trinity of great pediatricians in the Radford area where I grew up. Each trip to the doctor produced very little information other than it was... possibly... allergies.

As I would sit in the back seat of our family car on the way home, I could hear bits and pieces of my parents' conversation. The expression of exasperation started with *"what's wrong with him?"* followed by my mother expressing her concerns over *"if something ever happened to him..."* and then my father expressing frustration over the cost. I can remember feeling bad about being a burden on them. Often times, I would try and hide when I wasn't feeling well, but my wheezing and coughing would give me away.

Then, toward the end of my kindergarten year, there was the night in which I simply could not breathe. I sat in my mom's lap for hours begging her to help me breathe. She would walk me outside on the front porch to take in fresh air, but I simply could not get any in me. At that time, we only had one car and my dad was at work. By the time he got home, it was very late and I was rushed by them to the emergency room.

I don't remember everything that transpired once I arrived at the hospital, but it was serious enough that I was sent to see a specialist in Roanoke to figure out what was going on. A few days later, that specialist gave me fifty-two shots (twenty six in each arm) to test for every possible allergy. Turns out, I was allergic to the world.

The test results came back that I was allergic to all fifty two items tested. For the first time in my life, I understood what fear was. Everything outside the front door of our house could cause me to stop breathing. Certain foods could cause me to stop breathing. I was so confused and afraid. I was very limited in what I could do as a child because so many things could trigger a serious asthma attack.

Over the next several years, I was required to visit my doctor's office twice a week, usually right after school, and get two shots (one in each arm) that were meant to build my immune system and protect me from having any serious allergy attacks. To be honest, I overcame my fear of shots pretty quickly. When you have to have them that often and administered by a nurse who had the forearms of Popeye, you learn to take a deep breath, look away, close your eyes and simply endure. As I got older, I became brave and would just stick my arm out and say *"do it"*!

However, something inside me began to cower from enjoying the benefits of being a boy with friends playing outside. Most of my days were spent playing with my Star Wars toys or my electric football game in my bedroom while my younger brother and our friends played football outside. I can remember looking out my second floor bedroom window into my backyard and watching Keith, David, Kevin, Mike, Dale and others playing tackle football. I wanted to play too... but I held back.

At first, I held back because I was not healthy enough to go outside and play. I wanted to be healed of the asthma that kept me from going outside to play, but did not yet understand the power of prayer. Then, on a Sunday night church service, Pastor Briggs taught on healing. At the end of the service, he asked if anyone wanted to come up front to be prayed for and to receive healing. James 5:14 says *"Is anyone among you sick? Let them call the elders of the church to pray over them and anoint them with oil in the name of the Lord."* Now, I did not understand that an elder was a part of the church governing body. I thought *"elder"* meant old, and boy did we have enough older people at our church who were up front ready to pray! Without even asking permission, I went up to the altar to be prayed for, believing that God was going to heal me.

You know what? He did! Amen!

I began to proclaim my healing to all my family and friends. I physically felt better and truly believed that God had healed me. After a month, an appointment was made to see the same specialist in Roanoke. Once again, I was given 52 shots, 26 in each arm. However, this time, I was not allergic to any of them! I can remember both my parents looking at each other, and then me, in disbelief at what they were hearing from the doctors there. I was given a clean bill of health!

A new world had opened for me. I was now allowed to go outside to run, jump and play with my friends. Many of those days were lazy... playing in the dirt, building forts, riding our bikes and a million other things that boys used to get into before the age of video games. I was good with that, because it required nothing more from me than to just play.

As I got older, many of us began to get into sports. Like most boys, I enjoyed playing basketball and baseball, but our favorite was tackle football!

Now, I had always envisioned myself a great athlete. However, the truth of the matter was that I was, at best, average at anything I did athletically. My body was not as strong or muscularly developed as many of the other boys my age. My younger brother was taller and much bigger than I was at 14 (he was 13). I would not say that I was scrawny, but I simply was not as strong, as fast or as *"intense"* as most other boys in the neighborhood.

The most feared was Dwayne Rash. He was a beast. His muscles had muscles and he had the confidence of a warrior... a champion. Dwayne loved to talk trash, only as boys know how to do, to make sure everyone knew he was the Alpha Dog in Orchard Hills. I think most boys were a little intimidated by him. After seeing my brother and our friends tackling each other... throwing one another to the ground... it scared me. I especially cringed when I watched Dwayne go and tackle someone. There was a different sound to it. The victims got up a little slower and had a look of pain in their eyes.

I was scared of getting hit, to get thrown to the ground, and I was especially scared to experience that pain. I made excuses so I could be the quarterback for both teams! I would play sick or look for any excuse to not play. Simply put... I was afraid. Worst... Dwayne knew it. And, he let me know that he knew it, which made my struggle worse.

Fear is a very powerful emotion and, if not properly managed by us, it can cripple us to the point that we can never experience all that God wants for us. Fear becomes a problem if it gets out of control in our life. We must learn to rule over fear the same we must learn to rule over all of our emotions. John 10:10 says that Jesus came that we might have and enjoy life!

Fear is aroused by a threat that is either real or imagined. In my case, the threat of being hit while playing football was very real. However, the thoughts of having bones broken or my head decapitated by Dwayne Rash (which I dealt with almost every day it seemed) were imagined, but man did it ever feel real to me! Every time the boys from the neighborhood came to our house to ask Keith and me to play football, fear would overcome me and I would make every excuse in the book to try and get out of it. Basically, I would lie.

We have an enemy, and his name is Satan. Satan thrives on fear. His purpose is to steal, kill and destroy. Every day, he looks for opportunities to destroy our faith. If he can accomplish that in my life, or your life, or anyone's life, then he successfully stops us from performing God's will for our lives. Our purpose is stolen through fear. It will keep you from doing even the simplest tasks like swimming in a lake or driving a car on the freeway.

As a young teenager, I had faced fear many times: walking into kindergarten, getting all those shots, my first trip to the principal's office, giving my first public speech in sixth grade and talking to a girl on the phone. Those were easy compared to the fear I had facing Dwayne and the boys from the neighborhood. Looking back thirty years later, I think this was one of the most defining moments in my development as a young man. Everyone has fears they must face daily. However, we all have those defining moments in which we either face the fear that cripples us head on, or we cower away.

I knew in my heart that I did not want to be a coward. However, I also knew that I did not want to be decapitated by one of Dwayne's vicious hits. I was conflicted with the reality that I could hide in the house and be safe, or go outside those walls and face my fears.

On one particular rare evening when my dad was not working second shift, I was with him in the basement just piddling around when I came across this very little trophy. It was maybe five inches tall and no more than an inch and a half around. He explained that he got that trophy when he was in 8th grade while playing for his school's team. I sat, wide-eyed, as he told the story of his final game that year playing in the rain and mud with a chance to finish the season undefeated. He remembered like it was on TV yesterday. They lost the game 2-0 on a safety on the last play of the game.

That story opened the door about why I did not like to play football. Now, to know my dad is to know that he was a man's man and (at least in my eyes) he was afraid of nothing! Honestly, he bit the ear off a dog one time that attacked him in our neighborhood... or so the legend goes. However, here is his oldest son who was consumed with fear. I was afraid to get hit, to get thrown to the ground, to experience pain. As a result, I could not bring myself to enjoy the game as it seemed he did and all my friends were now.

We sat down and talked about a story from the Bible that I had heard many times growing up in church: David and Goliath. I'm sure many of you know that story found in I Samuel 17 (go look it up!). Basically, the Philistine army had this 10-foot giant named Goliath who was challenging God's chosen people, Israel, to send one soldier out to fight him. Of all the soldiers in Israel, no one came out to fight. Not one! As my dad explained 'ol Goliath was a trash talker because he believed he was invincible. Those in the

Philistine army would hoop and holler and cheer for him, because they believed he could not be defeated. This went on day, after day, after day.

Then, one day, David's father sent him to where Israel's army was encamped so that he could check on his brothers. When David arrived, he heard 'ol Goliath and his trash talking. He saw the fear in his brother's eyes, the other soldiers' eyes and even in the king's eyes. It seemed like everyone was consumed with fear. But, David told the king he would fight Goliath.

Now, here is where my dad gave me both the wisdom of how to face my fear and then the encouragement to go and actually face my fears. My dad looked me deep in my eyes and asked me to tell him the story. First, I told him that David had confidence because he had once fought off and killed a lion and a bear. Secondly, I told him that David was given the king's armor to put on, but it didn't fit right and it was too heavy. My dad nodded. Next, I told him that David went to the river bed, picked up three stones, and then prayed. Finally, he went out to meet Goliath face-to-face. Goliath made fun of David and insulted him. Meanwhile, David proclaimed an impending victory that God was about to deliver through him. Everyone there watched. David put a stone in the sling, twirled it around, and let it go. Next thing you know, Goliath had a stone hit him right between the eyes and down he went.

When I was done, my dad looked me in my eyes and told me that I was just like David. I had once fought off an illness that was intended to kill me when I was a boy. I faced the fear of 52 shots, the weekly trips for more shots. Through it all, my faith had grown to the point that I went up for prayer and received my healing!

Next, my dad said that I should be like David and not try to be something that I am not. The armor the king wanted David to wear was for soldiers. God used David's faith to defeat the enemy. Therefore, my dad told me that I should not be focused on how strong or how fast Dwayne was, but rather put faith in my ability to face him. If I continued to put my faith in God, He would bring me through any challenge. God would give me what I need in that moment to face my fear.

Finally, my dad said this to me. There is a time to pray and there is a time to prepare. If I really wanted to overcome my fear of playing football, I would need to get my head right, give my fear to the Lord and go and face it. End of story. Then, my dad left me with this: Fear and faith cannot exist in the same place.

We must understand that faith is a practical expression of confidence in God and His Word. In my mind, I struggled with how God would want to help overcome my fear about playing backyard football. Then, I found a scripture in Isaiah 41:10 *"So do not fear, for I am with you; do not be dismayed, for I am your God. I will strengthen you and help you; I will uphold you with my righteous right hand."* I was still very young in my faith, but I believed with all my heart that God would be with me if I decided to cross the street on Shepard Drive and walk into that field that was the home of those now famous backyard football games. I prayed that He would protect me and give me the courage to face my fears and, especially, Dwayne Rash.

A few weeks later, on a Saturday morning in October 1984, there was a knock on the door. It was some of the boys from the neighborhood looking for Keith and me to play football. To my dismay, Dwayne was standing at the door with them and, right off the bat, he began to mock me with the famous clucking noises that many of us hear when our manhood is challenged. I remember that overwhelming feeling of dread that came over me, but I was determined to go. I could hear my father's voice reminding me that fear and faith can not exist in the same place. Today was my day to face the fear.

I went into my room and changed into some appropriate clothing and then took a moment to read Isaiah 41:10 one more time. *"So, do not fear, for I am with you."* I knew God was going to be with me. *"Do not be dismayed, for I am your God."* I could almost hear God telling me not to be intimidated. *"I will strengthen you and help you."* It was like God was giving me a nudge to head on out and take care of business. I tied up my tennis shoes and jogged out the door and across the street with the same confidence that I can only imagine David had walking out to meet Goliath.

Very early in the game, it was obvious that Dwayne had bad intentions. He was hitting harder and slinging people down with more force than I could ever remember. I tried to tackle him a couple of times by grabbing his sweatshirt, but it was of no use. For a moment, I felt that I just wanted to survive and go home.

Then, on our next drive toward our makeshift endzone, Dwayne started the trash talking and focused mainly on me. As my team huddled up, I looked at Danny and said *"throw me the ball"*. I think this shocked everyone that new me. I walked up to the line and waited. *"Hut! Hut!"* I took about five steps and turned around. Danny delivered a nice, tight spiral into my gut. As I caught it, I was determined. With all of the faith and courage I could muster, I turned up field and started to run. I believe it was Kevin that grabbed my leg, but it was Dwayne coming at me with every intention of taking me out. I got free of Kevin and, in a moment of pure faith, I ran full steam at Dwayne and lowered my shoulder.

Looking back, what happened next truly changed my life. You see, I survived.

I got up off the ground and the first thing I heard was some of my friends offering words of encouragement, as only boys can, while walking back to the huddle. This apparently offended Dwayne and the trash talking intensified. He wanted another shot at me with the promise I would *feel it* this time. I walked back to the huddle.

Give me the ball, I said again. I walked back to the line.

This time, it was just me and Dwayne. And when I caught the ball, I was met with one of the most vicious hits I ever had or would ever endure. It hurt. It took a moment to get my bearings. I got up and walked back to the huddle. This time, I looked at Dwayne and smiled. I had taken what he had to offer... but the fear was gone!

Once again, in the huddle, I looked at Danny and said (a little louder) throw me the ball. Dwayne heard it too. Game on. Everyone just gave us space and the play developed with just Dwayne and I going head to head. This time, I delivered a stiff arm that sent him to the ground and I broke free to score a touchdown! My team celebrated the fact that I was really playing the game as much as the fact that we had scored.

After the game, Dwayne and I walked off the field friends. I look back now and realize just how much that moment in time helped me to face many other fears in life that I would face.

I believe that God wants to use moments like this to grow our faith. The question is this, are you ready to face your fears? If so, just know that God will be with you and He wants to help you overcome the enemy and his tactics. All you need to do is prepare your mind through His Word, pray and put your faith in Him!

ABOUT CHRIS BLACKBURN

Chris Blackburn is currently the Director of the R.O.C.K. Club children's program at the Radford Worship Center. The R.O.C.K. Club provides individualized, Christ-centered care to each child who attends the program. Chris and his wife, Tina, are also the Children's Pastors at the Radford Worship Center. Chris begin serving in children's ministries in 2000 as a leader in Royal Rangers and, later, serving as Pastor over Life Change JV, a pre-teen youth ministry.

Chris has a passion for young people that took flight in 2001 when he was hired by Premier, A School Specialty Company's Planning and Student Development division as a Sales Consultant to schools in Virginia, West Virginia, Kentucky and Tennessee. His consulting work helped implement programs into schools that included *"The 7 Habits of Highly Effective Teens"*, *"The Leader In Me"* and *"The Go Program"* among others. Twice, Chris was named to the President's Club by Premier for achieving higher than projected sales goals.

Chris has been invited on an annual basis since 2010 to be a key speaker at the Virginia Future Business Leaders of America summer conference.

Chris's passion is to help people achieve their potential through encouragement, vision and through their faith in God. He believes that the best way to achieve this is to be honest, but in a loving way.

Contact Chris:
- Website: www.RockClubVA.com
- Email: 19ChristopherBlackburn@gmail.com
- Phone: 540-835-9330

A CHANGED LIFE
By Tom Cain

A CHANGED LIFE

My dad owned a gas station back in the day when they used to wash windshields. I worked, as soon as I was tall enough. I was probably ten years old. We had great times together. After the accident at Kraft, I became a REALTOR®. I was working with my dad's real estate company from 1989 until 1993. My sister Traci moved back from Baltimore to run dad's office. Even though it was a family firm, we had other agents. Because I was so driven to succeed, I rapidly became the main producer for the office. I made the decision that I could no longer be the big fish in a little pond. I needed to be the minnow in a large lake.

I had learned so much from working with my dad and felt as if I was ready to move on. So I left my dad's company. I said dad, *"I've learned everything I can here. I need to learn even more."* He taught me integrity and to be honest. He was my role model and I looked up to him. So in 1993 I headed over to RE/MAX. He was upset but respected my decision. I hated the thought of my dad being upset or disappointed with me but I knew that I needed to grow in my profession. I chose to have courage to do what was best for me and trust that dad would understand and be happy for me. I felt like this was the right time to move forward.

Ecclesiastes 3:1 *"There is a time for everything, and a season for every activity under the heavens."*

I remember a time when dad was living down in Florida. He thought that my brother Tim and I were both very busy and not coming to visit for his 75th birthday. The rest of the family was celebrating inside a waterside restaurant. Tim went in first, and dad was so excited that he made it after all. He was so surprised. I waited about two minutes and then walked in hollering a big *"Ho, Ho, Ho"* the way he'd heard *"Ho, Ho, Ho"* for the last 25 years. He couldn't see me, but he knew it was me. He grabbed his chest above his heart. I thought he was going to have a heart attack; he was so happy. There was my dad, tears falling down his face. I just went up and hugged him and told him how much I loved him. It was a day I'll never forget. Imagine the love my dad has for me and how much more love our heavenly father has for us.

I remember the day that mom and I went to my dad's doctor appointment. I rode my Segway over, from about 4 miles away right into the hospital. Dr. Vasireddy said, *"I've been able to review everything and I just want to you know that you have stage four lung cancer."* Fear of losing my father set in. A fear came over me and consumed me. Fear of losing a parent is a horrible feeling.

Joshua 1:9 *"Have I not commanded you? Be strong and courageous. Do not be afraid; do not be discouraged, for the Lord your God will be with you wherever you go."*

I knew that I needed to be strong in spite of my fear. At that time I tried to be strong and not let the fear consume me. I needed to be strong for my dad that was sick and for my mom that was fearing of losing her husband.

Mom and dad left the room, and I stayed to talk with the doctor. I knew we had a lot of planning to do and decisions to make. I was also scheduled to speak at a Star Power Conference in Washington, DC, six weeks later. I asked the doctor if I should cancel? He said to me, *"Tom, you know, it's really hard to know how long this will take. It is terminal, but you know, you got to live your life."* Five weeks later, dad was back in a hospital and fighting terrible pain because the cancer was eating his vertebras and other parts of his body. We were trying to find a pain medication that would work, but not knock him out, because we wanted him around, but not in pain, as long as possible.

While he was in the Carle Hospital that week, I would bring coffee to my dad at 5:30 every morning; great coffee, not hospital coffee. That Friday, Dr. Vasireddy met me outside dad's room. He said, *"Are you still planning on going to that conference? I remember that I told you it was okay to go."* I said, *"Yes, I do."* He said, *"I was wrong. Don't go."* Now fear came over me even greater. I knew things were getting a lot worse and so quickly. I gave dad his coffee and my dad's first words that morning were, *"Tom, you've got to get me home"*. I called in a lot of favors. I hired an ambulance to transport us. It was an emotion filled fifteen-minute ride that I will never forget. My emotions were everywhere.

We got home and his family room was set up like a hospital room. On Monday, it was a like a living visitation, hundreds of people came, friends and family, to say goodbye to my dad. Then at 7:20 p.m., Tuesday, October 9, 2007, he passed; six weeks from the day he was told he had fourth stage lung cancer. We had worked together, and we were best friends, I was heartbroken. My mom went over to my dad, took his diamond ring off his finger and put it on mine. I still have it and treasure it. I went outside crying and upset. I was hurting but I knew I had to be strong for my mom. I had fear of this day but I found courage to be strong for my mom and now I need to be strong for her now more than ever.

John 14:27 *"Peace I leave with you; my peace I give you. I do not give to you as the world gives. Do not let your hearts be troubled and do not be afraid."*

John 14:1-2 *"Do not let your hearts be troubled. You believe in God; believe also in me. My father's house has many rooms; if that were not so, would I have told you that I am going there to prepare a place for you?"*

Mom and I love people. My mom is a people pleaser. She was a postmaster in Savoy, Illinois. During Christmas week, she would get up at 3 in the morning, make coffee cake, slice fruit and then get to work by 5 am. She set it all out as a beautiful display like she would do for her family. She's always did things for other people, and she's always did it sincerely. That's why I think I like cooking so much, also because I watched people enjoy her food like crazy and enjoying what a wonderful person she is. My mom taught me that less was more.

My mom was the breadwinner of our house. If she wanted to take a trip to a postal convention, she did. If she wanted to buy things for her kids or her grandkids, she bought them. I told her one day when I was in my 20s, *"Mom quit buying me stuff. I love you anyhow. Just love me, and I'm going to love you for who you are."*

Since my dad died in 2007, my mom has never been the same. She is a very responsible person. She is probably the only person in our immediate family that has the best credit rating of all of us still through all the stuff she's been through. My mom and I do things together like go to movies or out to dinner. We're very close. She dealt with the fear of losing my dad and being alone but as she has found courage along the way and she has learned to be independent. She has been strong in the midst of missing him.

I looked up to my father and respected him. I miss him now that he is gone but I know he is no longer in pain and in a much better place. My father set a good example for me and taught me that you work hard for what you get. His example of hard work, love, integrity, honesty and many more is what has made me who I am today and I'm forever grateful.

Exodus 20:12 *"Honor your father and mother, that your days may be long in the land that the Lord your God is giving you."*

Proverbs 1:8 *"Hear, my son, your father's instruction, and forsake not your mother's teaching."*

The word of God clearly states to honor our parents. Even though it was hard losing my father I know that I have nothing to regret because he knew that I loved and respected him.

Proverbs 22:6 *"Train up a child in the way he should go; even when he is old he will not depart from it."*

My dad raised me to be a hard worker, to have integrity and honesty. Today I am still that person. I'm thankful that he is my dad.

I went through a time when I was angry and got in a lot of fights. I would get drunk and I wasn't a nice drunk. One particular night, I was at the bar with some friends and a guy spilled a beer on me and I said something that offended him. The next thing I knew; I was on the ground getting beat up. The left side of my face was a mess of cuts; my left eye was completely closed. My right eye was full of blood, and my lips were puffed up. When I sobered up, I decided that, if I was in a bar and happened to have a guy spill a beer on me, I'd apologize to that guy and buy him two more beers instead of getting in a fight with him. I was done fighting.

The doctor told me if I ever got hit in that left eye again, I'd lose my sight. I was fearful. Sometimes it takes things like this to happen in our life to wake us up. Fear consumed me. I did not want to ever be in that position again. God began to deal with me through the word about my temper, fighting and anger. I decided that was not the life style I wanted any longer.

Proverbs 16:32 *"He who is slow to anger is better than the mighty, And he who rules his spirit, than he who captures a city."*

Proverbs 15:1 *"A gentle answer turns away wrath, But a harsh word stirs up anger."*

Proverbs 19:11 *"A person's wisdom yields patience; it is to one's glory to overlook an offense."*

Ecclesiastes 7:9 *"Do not be quickly provoked in your spirit, for anger resides in the lap of fools."*

I have experienced many types of fear but in this chapter I chose to share my relationship between my father and the fear of losing my father. It is a fear that I will never forget. The fear of losing someone so close like a parent is a fear like no other. I knew I had to find courage to go on, not only for myself but for the strength of my mother.

With the help of God and the word of God, I was able to find courage and be the support my mother needed.

My mother and I have bonded more and became a lot closer since dad is gone. I spend a lot of time with her, do things with her and go on outings with her to make sure she isn't lonely and also because I love spending time with her. I shared the fear of getting hurt if I didn't change my ways. That's what I did. I changed my ways. God has done a work in my life for the better but I had to be willing to allow him to do the work. God is a gentleman. He won't force anything on you. You have to want it.

As I close this chapter, I am a changed man.

ABOUT TOM CAIN

Tom started his career in 1977 working for Kraft Foods in Champaign, IL. In 1985 he was offered the opportunity to take the Dale Carnegie course called Human Relation Skills. In 1990 he was asked to come back and become a graduate assistant for the course, which most people will do once or twice in their life; Tom did it for the next 20 years!

Tom then began his Real Estate career in Savoy, IL, working with his dad, TL, and his sister Traci, the office manager. He hit the ground running with 23 sales his first year, and in 2006 he was at his pinnacle in the real estate business with a staggering 501 homes closed.

Most of Tom's life has been dedicated to God and giving back to the community. He is the co-creator of Friends of Santa, an organization that gives toys, clothes and food to every child in the school district at Christmas. A strong Christian today, Tom shares a darker time when chasing success brought on his love for money, and that became his god. Within three years, Tom lost his wealth and fell into a deep depression. Fortunately, God didn't turn away from him, and he not only found his way back to God, but was blessed with new success.

Today, Tom Cain is one of the leading coaches for Realtors®, Mortgage Lenders, Insurance Agents and other small business owners.

Contact Tom:
- Website: www.OneMansSegueThroughLife.com
- Phone: 217-202-3136

LEAVE THE LIGHT ON...
By Janet DiTroia

LEAVE THE LIGHT ON...

Dear Readers:

There is a part of me that didn't want to write this chapter as I knew how painful it might be and I didn't want to stir up the emotions deep in my heart. So, it has taken much time on my part to even contemplate my thoughts and bring them to light for others to see. I know deep down lies the little child who once lived in tremendous fear with painful experiences about the past. I thought I really could feel safe putting on blinders to hide, but I did for too many years to count. By discussing these experiences, I thought I may have to relive all of the past pain, but the deeper part of me, the one that love and knows herself, is in a much better place to realize that remaining quiet does not help to love, nurture, respect and honor myself.

I now make this promise to share what has been hidden for so long in the hopes of helping other people who have lived similar experiences to be enlightened or even inspired to take steps of their own to embrace their deepest thoughts and feelings. My heartfelt wish is to bring a light of truth about my life and graciously offer a safe place for others to realize their own truth of their life experiences. For many years, I had been abandoning my true feelings—literally locking the door never to be opened. At the time, I thought I was doing my best in protecting myself by just sweeping the dirt under the proverbial carpet of life. Now, I have realized the lessons given to me were tremendous blessings in disguise. I had taken away the gifts that were so graciously bestowed upon me from our creator. After all, I am not a little girl anymore and, at this point in my life, it is time to unveil the misunderstandings and belief systems that helped me to live in a perpetual cycle of fear.

Do people really honor their true feelings? Or, do they hide them away so no one can see them, even their own true self. Suppressing feelings seemed like a safe thing to do as I wouldn't have to face some of the deepest emotional pain in dealing with all the underlying hurt, rejection and God knows what else. It seemed like the right thing to do at the time.

I hadn't realized the wisdom that has unfolded for me now, and honestly I just did the best I could to cope with all of the *"anguish"*. I now ask myself: *"Anguish, (or other feeling/emotion) how may I serve you? What is it you are trying to show/tell me?"*

> *I ask questions I never thought of so long ago,*
> *and thinking about the answers empowers me to look for*
> *the real truth about who I really am.*

For example, if I feel angry, I ask Anger *"How may I serve you?"* I take a few deep breaths and my answer easily comes. In that case, I was angry because everyone was offering their opinions and suggestions about what I *"could"* or *"should"* do in a particular situation. They don't understand how I feel, how could they? I know they are well intended, but they are giving their ideas based on *"their"* life experiences. They can only speak for themselves. I now know I think for myself and follow *"my own intuition."* People are always trying to help, so just saying thank you is enough and move on with what feels right in your heart. Trying to explain your thoughts to *"help"* them understand many times is a waste of your precious energy as they are not inside your body, mind or spirit, so they cannot truly have a sense of what is *"right"* for you. That's ok. We are all here on our own journeys.

In the next few paragraphs, I will detail some of my basic experiences just to give an understanding of the turmoil I experienced over the years, and to provide a foundation for this conversation which led to my healing journey.

Some details about the past...

I can clearly remember being bullied throughout some of my junior high school years and throughout all of high school years, not to mention the first year of college. That is a long time to be called names, emotionally berated, rejected by some peers and verbally brutalized to the point of no return. My spirit felt so diminished; I felt ugly, unacceptable to myself and others, and I wanted to hide under a rock and not be seen by anyone. Day after day, I did not want to get up to go school; I did not want to sit next to anyone (for fear of being pointed out, laughed at or listen to words that were so cruel, nasty and hurtful). I couldn't understand why they picked on me because I was a shy child who never provoked anyone, so why was I the butt of everyone's punishment? Sometimes it was more than one person saying nasty things. In fact, it was a group many times, and I was outnumbered and felt powerless. Those feelings of worthlessness perpetuated for a long time and I didn't know how to overcome such overwhelming odds.

I am thrilled to say I survived it! As many years came to pass, I did my best to maintain confidence in myself throughout my life experiences. I got married and raised three wonderful children who make me very proud. I also got divorced. So many relationships came and went. I am thankful for all them for they were my teachers, my friends and they helped to bring the light of truth about me to the surface.

Not until my mid-forties did I begin the journey of facing all the fear and emotional pain of the past. And, I committed to revealing my truth in the two books I wrote called *My Eyes are Open* and *My Heart is Open*. I am ready, willing and able to be my best me. I realized that self-expression is a truly a gift from our creator. I had resisted/feared being the *"real"* me. So, it is time to open the door, step through, acknowledge what really happened and take baby steps in moving forward towards healing my heart.

I now know that we are here to fully express ourselves with all the aspects of our emotions, whether it be happy, sad, angry, heartbroken, conflicted, anxious or something else. Most of us find it easy to talk about the beautiful and positive things that make us feel so good, but it's another level of courage to embrace the *"not so good stuff."* I find that many people are not effectively equipped to deal with the upsetting emotions.

In general, we don't often know how to express ourselves clearly and difficulty arises when we attempt to overcome circumstances, especially when our emotions can get the best of us. Self-expression is a very important key to opening the door of self-love. We do our best to manage and some of us do better than others. It is a constant unfolding of our true essence.

Think of how many people you know that take things *"to the grave"* and never really find resolution. They stand in fear of what or what not to do, so nothing gets resolved. I did not want to be one of those people. I wanted to feel happy, healthy, emotionally well-balanced and joyful for no apparent reason—just because that is our true nature. I had to take responsibility for my emotions. In that way, I could embrace what felt good and what did not.

Is all choice? So, why on earth do so many people choose unhappiness? Unconsciously, they are unaware of ability to change their thoughts which is where our true power lies. Now, I choose much differently—more in alignment with what makes me feel good. I would call that *"God Centered Thoughts."*

I know of people from my therapy practice that won't talk with their siblings because of *"something that has them"*. So they remain upset and no one discusses their feelings for fear of the *"perceived"* repercussions. So many relationships and families are broken apart by poor communication and inability to express true feelings. Why are we all so fearful?

I wonder how long we can walk down the dark hallway, in the tunnel of denial, telling ourselves its ok to sweep the dirty stuff under rug so that way no one will see it. How long can we do this? Do you do this? I've have managed to accomplish this for 45+ years. I can't say it doesn't bother me, because it eventually caught up with me. In fact, I think I had been lying to myself for reasons of Self-preservation and coping—so much fear of *"feeling the emotions"* and experiencing life fully. That is why we are here: to live life fully and completely.

Self-procrastination fears have a way of keeping us dead in our tracks to just exist without allowing ourselves to realize the truth and then to take steps to move on happily. I had to begin with being gentle, compassionate and loving to myself. I was never accustomed over the years to do that, so I had to start from scratch. I used mirror work to look right in my eyes and tell myself I was worth loving. I looked at pictures of me at age 14 up through college age, and told myself that I didn't deserve any of the cruelty or nastiness from any person, since I was such a loving person and had so much to offer in the world. I told myself, in no uncertain terms, that I deserved wonderful things, including loving relationships. I told myself everything I knew I needed to hear, in order to soothe my broken heart.

Those techniques, along with meditation, prayer, walks in the park, journaling and writing my books, really helped to heal, nurture and lovingly support this girl. For the first time in my life, I felt complete in every way. I began to notice things I did right, instead of my old conditioning that told me everything I did wrong. I noticed *"me"* in beautiful ways for the first time. I allowed all of emotions to come forward. I honored them completely then moved on as I felt guided to do so.

Although we are all doing our best given our understanding of the world and the people with whom we interact with in our life, it seems like it we (our culture) is now beginning to shift in our relationships and desires. We want to make changes, especially since the old paradigms (outdated ways of thinking) are not working anymore. I wonder what would help us to be better able to improve relationships with others. What do you think?

I have found our relationships with others all boils down to the relationship we have with ourselves.

This is so important that it bears repeating…

I have found our relationships with others all boils down to the relationship we have with ourselves.

I had to rebuild my relationship with the little girl, *"Janet"*. Eventually, I had to learn to be gentle, compassionate and loving to myself—as gentle as a mother would be to a 5 year old child. After all, we are fragile in our hearts and deserve only forgiveness, love and compassion. All these lessons are blessings here to help us remember our true divine and the essence of our loving self.

Not realizing these golden nuggets of wisdom at the time, I choose a more familiar path—the one I knew quite well which said *"You are not deserving or worthy. And, you are unacceptable as you are."* That's a difficult way to live day to day, but many of us do that unconsciously. These misunderstandings of our belief systems feel real and we are unknowingly robbing ourselves of self-esteem, overall well-being and happiness.

It takes a tremendous amount of courage/fearlessness to allow ourselves to feel our emotions, then acknowledge them fully, especially the painful ones. I found a way to hide by letting all the lies remain dormant in my heart. How do you overcome and rise above these hurtful words and actions when you are afraid? How to you go on each day feeling happy, loving, gentle and compassionate and honest with your deepest self?

My experiences have lead me to believe that we are not taught these things in typical school settings, and our parents and other mentors may not have had the luxury of these teachings as well. So we do our very best to embrace whatever experiences lie before us.

Some of our experiences are wonderful and some…not so much… It may just seem easier to allow ourselves to *"forget"* the bad stuff and just move on. I will say some people can do that effortlessly. But, the majority of us don't realize how delicately fragile in nature we are as human beings. People's words and actions can and do hurt and even devastate one's well-being.

I found it easier to not talk about it, forget it and stuff it down, so that way I could go on with my life. Hiding was safe. I wanted to be safe! I protected my heart, *No More Emotional Pain!* That was my mindset at the time. I now see things quite differently.

It is now time to open the door, tiptoe in and make our grand entrance. I am not hiding anymore, are you? I am becoming more and more aware of how I feel as I cross the bridge of life. Fear was very much my past. And, on occasion, it may show up now and then. But, I am much better equipped to handle whatever comes my way. I feel quite confident knowing I can make as many mistakes as I need to and I am not afraid to embrace how I feel.

Don't we owe it to ourselves to be honest?

I know and finally feel it is time to shine light on how bullying impacted my life from a young girl and into my forties. I was afraid to speak my mind and my heart, but now I am ready to move along. I have finally forgiven myself for denying myself the truth and feel SO relieved to honor this little girl, for she is worthy and deserves only the best that life can offer.

As Matt Kahn would say, send yourself *"More love not less."* Remember to look at yourself and say I love you often, for the little child within us all needs to know that she/he is strong, fearless and ready to embrace this wonderful life with heart-centered way of being. Never less, only more...

My deepest hope and prayer is that my experiences will touch others who have been impacted by being bullied or touch others who are the bullies. I am offering loving words and guidance for helping others to open their eyes and heart in seeing the real truth about who they are and how to rise above the pain that resides in their hearts.

We are resilient, fearless and powerful when we embrace our natural state of being where we allow ourselves to always remember to *"leave the light on"* for...LOVE...

ABOUT JANET DITROIA

My mission is to embrace, love, acknowledge and empower every child as a unique expression of love, knowing that everyone of us has exquisite gifts to be brought forth in miraculous ways. As a conduit of God's loving light may I guide our own inner child and the children who grace our presence to embody the truth: that we all matter, and are magnificent beings here with passion and purpose to shine brightly with all our dreams. Embodying these words of wisdom help all of us to open the doors to become true leaders in a world created through the grace of love.

May we all walk together as one…

Contact Janet:
- Website: www.RecreateANewLife.com
- Facebook: www.Facebook.com/rich44
- LinkedIn: www.LinkedIn.com/in/JanetDiTroia
- Pinterest: www.Pinterest.com/janetditroia
- Email: jandit44@gmail.com
- Phone: 215-260-6036

THE GREAT EXCHANGE OF LOST AND FOUND

By Dave Frett

THE GREAT EXCHANGE OF LOST AND FOUND

I recall a childhood memory when wandering through the woods with my Dad during a pre-hunting season trip in which we would encounter an experience we were unprepared to tackle.

We were out scouting the area that we would soon be trekking across to hunt deer. We were searching for signs that would confirm we were in the best possible place to take home the prize we were so anticipating. Along with discovering signs of activity, we also sought the right place to set up our tree stand – trees that grew close enough together that would allow for a ladder and platform upon which to stake out our prey. However, having forgotten our compass, we trampled obliviously through the underbrush. Approximately a mile or so in, we realized we had failed to mark our way as best as possible and before long it seemed as if everything looked the same; in other words, we had lost our way.

As we had been out for a good portion of the day, we were now growing weary and hungry, needless to say that the sun was now in its departure process from the sky overhead, it was imperative that we either find our way out soon or make plans to spend the night. While our family had known the approximate area we had planned to inspect, no one would know with absolute certainty where we had ventured. Even though we had a rough idea of where we desired to be, the vagueness of our effort to backtrack our steps and the similarity of the landscape left us walking in circles and ever deeper into a lost state.

Before long, the sun would be completely erased from the sky overhead and the darkness of night would set in along with the impending temperature drop and the danger of nocturnal wildlife inhabitants. Being just a boy, the anxiety and fear that began to rear its ugly head that would cause me to worry and experience panic and trepidation of indefinite disorientation and a sense of being adrift in the wild outdoors, apart from a secure, warm environment at home with family, began to spin my mind, my eyes and my spirit into a sense of uncertainty of the present and apprehension for the future.

Would we have to spend the night in the cold, darkness of the forest? Would we manage to avoid harm and peril from the animals in the midst? Would others come looking for us? Would we ever find our way out? Question after question flooded my mind as we walked briskly and intentionally to the west praying with each step that God would direct our path and bring us to the light of day; praying that safety would be wrapped around us; praying that we would never again experience such a feeling of complete and utter isolation and insufficiency. As but a child, this was a fearful experience that produced all types of feelings that would be perceivable in the present, but which could also produce long-term side effects if not appropriately handled.

Being lost, whether hiking or driving, is a feeling that swings wide the door to insecurities, nervousness and agitation. When one is lost and no longer in control of his own situation, it elicits feelings of panic, self-doubt and vulnerability. The very act of being physically irretrievable, emotionally absent or spiritually forgotten can cause one to dwell on the past, live emotionless in the present and ponder the future with great uncertainty. For one to live without assurance of his position or a solid path; for one to wander hopelessly, always frightened by what lay around the corner; and for one to hope he can navigate his course without an unshakable map, will only leave him self-conscious and fearful instead of assertive and self-confident.

Fortunately for me and my Dad, we did not end up having to spend the night in the forest. After roughly another hour and a half of collecting our bearings and retracing our steps, along with the Lord's starry compass, we were able to return to the opening where we had initially parked the car. Though we were able to find our way back geographically, how many times in life have we found ourselves lost either realistically or metaphorically?

Even more so, how many a person has wandered and wondered discerning his condition of being eternally spiritually lost or his ability to ever know for certain that his lost days are long behind and gone? Many a person struggles with the fear of closing his eyes and waking in hell—the struggle with closure of knowing beyond a shadow of a doubt that his life has been saved and rescued for all eternity. The fear that though he may have always known about God and may have even *"walked an aisle"* or *"made a decision"*, still struggles with the fear of whether it was authentic, genuine and heart-based or whether it was simply intellectual, thus carrying no eternal significance and leaving him eternally lost, with no hope of rescue.

Fear of being lost, fear of being alone and fear of having made the wrong decision or the inaction of a decision are often laden and cumbersome upon the self-assurance and courage of many. This is an imperative obstacle for the Church to tackle and eradicate through the proper instructing of believers called discipleship. Turning this one fear of uncertainty into a foundation of fortitude and boldness would transform the Church and move believers from being spiritually ill to possessing a degree of godly conviction not yet revealed in modern time.

Imagine for a moment if you will, what it would be like every night to close your eyes and wonder if you were to never breathe another breath whether you would awaken for all eternity in heaven or if you would fall short and spend your eternity in the fiery flames of hell—all because you wondered whether you truly knew Christ as Savior. Now imagine all of those who become so paralyzed in their fear that they are constantly anxious, questioning their eternal destination, to the level that they fail to grow in their faith, they regularly miss out on experiencing spiritual victories and they flounder to share their conviction in the life-giving blood of the cross because of their own infancy of faith. When one cannot even take solace and have peace in his own eternal destination, knowing he is no longer eternally lost but saved and rescued for all time to come, how can he share with another this precious blessing from above?

A.W. Tozer once noted, *"If man had his way, the plan of redemption would be an endless and bloody conflict. In reality, salvation was bought not by Jesus' fist, but by His nail-pierced hands; not by muscle but by love; not by vengeance but by forgiveness; not by force but by sacrifice. Jesus Christ our Lord surrendered in order that He might win; He destroyed His enemies by dying for them and conquered death by allowing death to conquer Him."*

Fear of being eternally lost; fear of landing at the footstep of Heaven only to be turned away; fear of having known in one's mind the factual information relevant to eternal freedom but not having applied it to a heart-filled, realistic decision in Christ's ability to save and hold instead of his own are fears that chase and corrode the mind and spirit of believers of all ages and spiritual maturity. Whereas for many, it would seem that the fear which is produced in the questioning of one's eternal destiny is rooted in the fear that what one has done is beyond the saving, forgiving grace of an Almighty God. However, Charles Spurgeon once addressed this when he wrote, *"It is not thy hold on Christ that saves thee; it is Christ. It is not thy joy in Christ that saves thee; it is Christ. It is not even thy faith in Christ, though that be the instrument; it is Christ's blood and merit."* When the fear of one's eternal destiny is removed because he employs the truth that salvation is rooted in Christ and not himself, the fear will be released and replaced with a courage that says' *"Whatever comes my way in Him I can tackle it."*

Recalling that day where I was lost in the woods and drawing a correlation to a spiritual experience, I lacked purpose, security and direction because I had no focus. Simply, I was lost; but more than being lost, it was the fear of being lost that truly plagued me. Many believers today are plagued in their minds and hearts as to whether they are saved or lost; not because Jesus is incapable of saving but because the enemy has learned how to attack those who have spent their lives in Church. While he knows that he cannot cause a believer to become unsaved, if he can cause him to doubt his salvation, he prevents his growth and ultimately his influence. Additionally, the enemy attacks the mind of a believer in regard to his state of salvation by challenging him to ponder, *"How can you commit such sins and not be lost?"* or attempting to cause him to think, *"Have I ever really believed in my heart or do I just understand and accept it academically?"* To this point David Jeremiah commented, *"Don't let obstacles along the road to eternity shake your confidence in God's promise. The Holy Spirit is God's seal that you will arrive."*

Believers struggle with the fear of eternal redemption and salvation; believers grapple with the thought of possibly being lost; and believers wrestle with the certainty of a heart relationship with God instead of just an intellectual understanding – not of any fault on God's behalf but because we have failed to become engrained in the Word and our personal discipleship. Much like it would have prevented my Dad and me from becoming lost had we had a compass, as believers we can be sure of not being lost if we would simply open our spiritual compass – the Word. Indeed, John once wrote, *"I write these things to you who believe in the name of the Son of God that you may know that you have eternal life"* (I John 5:13). One does not have to live in a state of fear or feel perplexed about his eternal providence – he can know beyond a shadow of a doubt that he is no longer lost. The fear of being lost can become a spot in the rear view mirror instead of being a heap on the windshield of life.

Fears can be debilitating; they can cause one to always be looking in the rear view mirror, dwelling upon past mistakes or they can propel one to look ahead, anticipating ruin and disaster, thus missing out on the present joys and experiences. Fear often extinguishes and prevents courage, making it an imperative issue to tackle and eradicate from one's life. Keeping this in mind, there have been many acronyms for FEAR over the years, but two that I believe, sum up the absolute different and distinct directions that one can pursue are viewing FEAR as (1) *False Evidence Appearing Real* or (2) *Face Everything And Rise.*

With regard to the first – many times individuals worry about and fear situations that never come to fruition. Too much time is spent fearing the possible circumstances or having an inappropriate perspective of current events, all of which could be removed with the correct and proper information or perspective. We seem to manufacture our own outcome based upon the skewed lenses we choose to view from; when as believers, we should be testing each situation against the Word of God.

To the second option, that which follows more in the desired steps of a Christian Warrior, removing fear is standing strong in the face of it through the power of Christ. The fear and worry of one being eternally lost is real and damaging but one that can be overcome. Indeed, John MacArthur once noted about the power of eternal salvation as, *"Saving faith is not just believing that Jesus lived and died. Faith that saves is the confident, continuous confession of total dependence on, and trust in Jesus Christ to meet the requirements on your behalf to give you entrance into God's Eternal Kingdom. It's the surrender of your life in complete trust to Him to do what you cannot do."*

Fear is a tremendous emotion for it can either cause one to possess and a command a spirit of flight or fight. Fear can cause one to either run, back down and, figuratively or realistically, curl up in hope that the component causing the alarm or trepidation will simply pass by or it can cause the individual to stand up, facing the angst and order his steps. Fear does not have to have a negative connotation; in fact, many times God chooses to use fear to teach, develop and even, protect His children. Fear is at times used to establish boundaries, helping to protect one from possibly unfavorable, adverse or even deadly consequences. While at others times, fear is used to draw one closer to God, helping to develop trust and vision in One greater than ourselves; regardless the reason, fear is not to dominate our lives. Indeed the Bible encourages us in II Timothy 1:7, *"For God has not given us a spirit of fear and timidity, but of power, love and self-discipline."*

The truth is no one enjoys experiencing fear – whether real or fabricated. Fear often drains our resolve, can cause anxiety, it creates an overwhelming pit in our stomach, sweaty palms and a head full of uncertainty and fear can even bring one to tears and great remorse. However, fear can also cause one to demonstrate a strength and commitment that he never knew could be mustered.

The challenge to defeating any fear and instead experiencing courage is accomplished in facing the fear in question. Much of this can be achieved through research, study and preparation and questioning. The Word of God has much counsel to provide with regard to fear.

From a positive standpoint, the Word exhorts in Proverbs 9:10, *"Fear of the LORD is the foundation of wisdom. Knowledge of the Holy One results in good judgment"* while Proverbs 1:7 depicts, *"Fear of the Lord is the foundation of true knowledge, but fools despise wisdom and discipline."* So from the aspect of fearing, or maintaining a high reverence toward an Almighty God and growing in knowledge, fear is a positive attribute – it allows us to understand that we are not the end all, but that there is One greater than us who can lift us up, restore us and supply our every need - but to whom we will also answer.

Indeed, Elisabeth Elliot once noted, *"Fear arises when we imagine that everything depends on us."* On the other hand, we are reassured over and over again, *"Be strong and courageous. Do not be afraid; do not be discouraged, for the LORD your God will be with you wherever you go"* (Joshua 1:9). Fear is an instrument used by the enemy to strip us of the power and confidence we can possess in every situation not because of who we are but because of Whose we are.

There is no need to fear whatever the trial may be; but with all certainty and knowledge, one need not fear the idea of being lost, either temporarily or eternally. Jesus implored his followers in John 14:27, *"Peace I leave with you; my peace I give you. I do not give to you as the world gives. Do not let your hearts be troubled and do not be afraid."* This promise still rings true for us today! The reason He was able to encourage those who heard His words, and for those who hear His words today, is because of the overarching ability of God to keep those who have become His.

To this point, Jesus emboldened His followers in John 10:28-30 when He implored, *"I give them eternal life, and they will never perish. No one can snatch them away from me, for my Father has given them to me, and he is more powerful than anyone else. No one can snatch them from the Father's hand."* Therefore, our rescue, our protection and our salvation is not because of us and is not dependent upon us – it is, and has always been, through Christ.

Today, when I head out on the road for a trip, whether near or far, the first thing I do is to access the directions (usually Googling it on my phone). The reason for this is so that I am aware of which direction to advance, so that I know when I need to turn so as to avoid making wrong decisions, to be cognizant of detours or obstacles that may arise in my path and ultimately to prevent myself from getting lost. This is what the Word of God is designed to do for our spiritual lives. It provides guidance, knowledge and security so that we may have confidence we are on the right path and will find ourselves successfully to our desired destination.

Unlike that day in the woods when I was afraid, lost and uncertain as to whether I would find my way home, there is no need to be hesitant or unsettled about one's eternal destination. Stop fearing the idea of being eternally lost. Get in touch with the Survival Guide. Establish a path that comes with an exit plan. And then live life with courage and confidence, believing whatever may come has already been resolved in the portals of eternity by the One Who knows and secures your every step.

Today, EXCHANGE FEAR FOR COURAGE. EXCHANGE LOST FOR FOUND.

REGAIN YOUR LIFE.

ABOUT DAVE FRETT

Greetings and Salutation.

My name is Dave Frett. I am a husband, father and author, but most of all, a disciple of Christ. I was raised in a Christian home and had the privilege of being introduced to Christ at a young age where I accepted Him as my personal Savior. Over the course of my life, I have experienced highs and lows just as any other believer living in a sin-infested world and a corrupted body; however, through it all God has never given up on me.

Today I desire to be a present *"voice shouting in the wilderness, 'Clear the way for the LORD's coming!'"*. We are living in turbulent times where believers are sinking in the mire instead of standing on the Rock. We are in need of hearing the Lord's anthem heralded from the courts of Heaven. And we are in need of understanding where we stand so that once again we may begin living as victors in Christ! Please join me in pleading to God for our families, our churches and our nation so that we may claim His promise and realize our worth in Him.

"For God has not given us a spirit of fear and timidity, but of power, love and self-discipline." - II Timothy 1:7

Contact Dave:
- Website: www.BattlestrongMinistries.com
- Facebook: www.Facebook.com/TheBattleIsReal
- Email: DavidFrett@aol.com
- Phone: 609-709-4967

FREEDOM FROM FEAR IN COURAGE TO FORGIVE

By Lydia Gates

FREEDOM FROM FEAR IN COURAGE TO FORGIVE

As I have grown and matured into the young woman I am today, I sometimes look back on how life has treated me. Most memories I have consist of the good times shared with my closest friends and the family trips we took across the oceans. But, some I keep locked away in the back of my mind seldom being remembered, but nonetheless ever present. These memories are what made me who I am.

At a young age, I learned to understand what cruel meant and what it felt like. When you're young, you don't understand what normal is or what normal should look like. With this in mind, I never knew that I was different. I never knew that *"what I said was any different from what others said"* and that *"the way I looked was any different from the way they looked."*

I tried my hardest as a young girl to fit in. I was very over weight and insecure. I didn't look like a lot of the girls my age and I was picked on a lot for it by my peers. The only thing I wanted to do was be accepted and loved for who I was.

I tried to make friends the best I could and the ones I chose were based on what I thought was the cool crowd. Everyone wanted to be friends with them, but few made the cut. I didn't want to be seen as the girl who had lame friends because I know how looked down upon those *"lame"* friend groups were and I was too prideful to be seen with the lame crowd. Because of this desire to be with the *"it crowd"* of cool people, I set aside what I knew were friendly characteristics and pursued the *"it crowd."*

The first chance I got, I befriended one of the girls who belonged in the *"it crowd."* Before long, I had become well-liked by most of them, or so I thought. I thought it was mostly because of how much I made them laugh. I loved talking to them and being part of their conversations. They always talked about what was going on in everyone's lives, even if they didn't know those people personally. Hanging out with them was great most of the time. I always felt like I had a place to go and people to tell my jokes to.

My closest friends at the time liked to laugh—I didn't know it then, but it was mostly at me. I didn't really understand at the time that I was the designated butt of their jokes. I don't remember what the jokes were or who told them, but I remember the feeling they gave me when they were said. The jokes hurt my self-esteem and made me realize that I was different.

It surprised me that these people, whom I'd come to care about and who meant everything to me, could turn against me so savagely without me even recognizing it. I began to think that maybe I had chosen the wrong friend group, but I didn't put too much thought into it. Not many people can say they are a part of this group, so I never said much to defend myself. I just stayed to myself and would laugh along with their jokes, as if they didn't bother me.

Things began to escalate as the year passed, and I became overwhelmed with the thought of never being accepted. I knew deep down that these people didn't really want to be with me and I was kept there for a *"go-to knee-slapper"*. It had gotten to the point where it was impulsive for me to be around them, so I wouldn't be alone. It would seem like that would be the opposite of what I wanted to do, but I didn't have anywhere to go. I constantly followed my *"friend"* group around, in hopes no one would think I was a loner.

The more obsessive I became about not being alone, the more my self-esteem suffered due to my friends harsh ways of communication. But, for some reason, I couldn't leave. I wasn't confident enough to be able to stand alone. I couldn't, for the life of me, separate myself and say *"the way you treat me is wrong, and I will not surround myself with people who hurt me."*

I was constantly convincing myself that it was okay for them to pick with me and to say those things because they were *"just having fun"* right? I started believing that it was my fault they treated me this way, like I had done something wrong.

I decided to tell them I was sorry, for what I didn't know, but I had to try something. I made the decision that I needed to apologize, so I went to them one day and told them I was sorry if I had ever hurt them. I genuinely tried to make things right. I remember distinctively asking them *"Will you forgive me"*? They said: *"No!"* They would never forgive me, because I was unforgivable. This was my first memory of forgiveness.

Being told I was unforgivable was the worst feeling I had ever had. It was extra baggage I constantly carried around that would only weigh me down. Knowing my mistakes would always be thrown back into my face and never forgotten had hurt more than anything. It was almost a downward spiral from there.

As middle school rolled around, things were even worse. The good news: I had left that friend group and now I was alone. I hated being alone. I wanted someone to notice me and to be friends with me. I took matters to the extreme and began cutting myself. Most people, who do this, say they do it because the pain inside of them has to be released or that cutting is the only thing they can control. Those were two of the reasons I would do this, but I mainly wanted someone to see how much my heart hurt from being alone and being hopeless.

This went on for a year, until my life changed.

After a year of this hopelessness, I knew there was something I needed—something I was missing.

I had been going to church for most of my life. Not every Sunday, but maybe once a month. I never really thought I needed to pay attention to what the man in the front was ranting about. How could he possibly know what I'm going through? It seemed that, after this whole ordeal with these people, I began to listen and try to understand what that man was talking about.

I was at the end of my rope and was running out of hope. Weeks went on and I began to ask my parents what it meant to be saved and why we should be saved. They would explain to me the importance of getting saved and having a personal relationship with God. On the contrary to what my friends had said, I could be forgiven, and by the most important person, Jesus. And my self-inflicted stripes could be healed.

One Sunday, we were visiting my grandma's church. I had made the decision that I had wanted to get saved, but I still didn't know when and where or really how I would do it. They had a visiting preacher from out of state who reached out to me during his sermon. I honestly don't remember what he preached on or what he prayed about. Near the end, he asked everyone if they would bow their heads. He said, *"If anyone here today is unsure of where they'd go if they died today, would you mind raising your hand?"* I paused, and raised my hand without realizing it.

After this, he asked the ones who raised their hands to say a prayer with him while we were standing. As I said this prayer and gave my heart to God, I felt that all those things that those people had said to me were lifted off my shoulders. I don't know how many people raised their hands that day, but I wasn't the only one who was saying that prayer. It was like a chorus of voices was saying it with me. He then asked for everyone who said the prayer to come forward and he looked at me, only me.

After that day, I knew that what they had said about me being unforgivable was untrue. I had been forgiven and my sins would be remembered no more.

A month later I was baptized on September 7, 2014. That week at school, those friends that hurt me from so long ago congratulated me.

Since then, everything hasn't been easy. Not even close. Temptation waits around every corner. The way is straight yes, but it has its ups and downs. Growing up in a world full of *"self-hate and hating thy neighbor"* is difficult.

It took me a long time to find the LOVE that I so desperately needed and to understand what it looked like. The best way I have found to sum it up would be 1st Corinthians 13:4-8,

Love is patient
Love is kind.
It does not envy,
it does not boast,
it is not proud.
It does not dishonor others,
it is not self-seeking,
it is not easily angered,
it keeps no record of wrongs.
Love does not delight in evil but rejoices with the truth.
It always protects, always trusts, always hopes, always perseveres.
Love never fails.

When I found these verses, I made a point to remember them. I know now WHAT I WAS MISSING BEFORE WAS LOVE. I didn't love myself. Now when I doubt God's love, I say these verses and know that He loves me always. I recall this verse anytime I am angry at my friends or myself—anytime I see someone else with something I want or anytime I become self-absorbed. With these verses, I can show someone the true love I wasn't shown those many years ago. I can be a light for someone's dark path that I never had.

In hindsight, I thank those people who hurt me. Without them, I may not have come to Christ because I wouldn't have felt like I needed something. Without them, I would have never discovered my calling to help people my age going through the same pain that I did.

Because of my experiences, I understand that forgiving others and loving them with a true agape love [the highest form of love, the love of God for man and of man for God] is what we should do for everyone. I know now how important it is to forgive those who have wronged us, because Christ forgives us no matter what we do. I know now how to love people because of how perfectly true love is summed up in 1st Corinthians 13:4-8. I don't hold grudges against them. I pray instead that they will have the same experience as I did when I asked Christ to forgive me.

I sometimes see them and the memories of what they said are seldom remembered, because I chose instead to remember when Christ forgave me and healed my stripes.

ABOUT LYDIA GATES

Lydia Gates lives in Lincolnton North Carolina and has a passion for literature and fine arts. In her spare time she plays clarinet and writes poetry.

Recently she was inducted into the Beta Society that represents her ability to be a leader in her school community.

Her continued hopes are to lead youth her age through life's challenges.

To have Lydia come and share her story with your organization reach out to her on Facebook at www.Facebook.com/Lydia.Gates.56 or email her at LydiaMGates@gmail.com.

Contact Lydia:
- Facebook: www.Facebook.com/Lydia.Gates.56
- Instagram: www.Instagram.com/Lydiaa.Marie
- Email: LydiaMGates@gmail.com

KEEP IN STEP WITH THE SPIRIT

By Chris McClure

KEEP IN STEP WITH THE SPIRIT

Since we live by the Spirit, let us keep in step with the Spirit.
- Galatians 5:25 (NIV)

In April 2016, I let go of the stability of a 17+ year career as a full-time pastor with a steady salary to step out in faith and into a business that I believed God was calling me to build. What led up to this massive shift? Let me take you on my personal journey to explain.

I was born into a Christian family that taught me about Jesus from my earliest memories. I was at a church camp when I was 12 years old when a friend asked me why I had never formally accepted Christ and been baptized. I didn't have a good answer, but knew it was the right next step to take in my faith. I went home, told my parents and was baptized the next Sunday. In the following years, I continued to grow and learn about following Jesus.

When I entered high school, I was fairly strong in my faith, but began to struggle for my independence as a typical teenager. At the age of 14, my grandfather died from his battle with a rare form of cancer. During his final weeks of life, I closely watched this man who was passionately committed to his family and his Lord. I remember thinking, *"I want my life to look like that."* His death was a devastating loss to our family, but his example was foundational in the man God was building in me. A lasting legacy had been created.

At the age of 16, reality hit me hard that I needed to figure out what to do with my life beyond high school. Each time a military recruiter called I said *"no,"* but I started to wonder if that was my best option. I didn't have a vision for my life. I was clueless and frustrated.

During my junior year of high school, my youth pastor asked me to consider going on a 17-day mission trip to Guyana, South America. I had no idea where this place was nor had I ever heard about it. All that I heard was *"17 days away from home."* I thought that would be good for me. I definitely didn't sign up for the trip with deep spiritual intentions. However, that didn't stop God from working powerfully in me.

While on the trip, God had my full attention. Stepping outside of your comfort zone makes you much more aware of your dependence on God! My youth pastor poured into our team and helped us think about how God might use us. I learned that God not only had a plan for me serving in a foreign country for those 17 days, but He also had a plan for me to serve back home. I finally felt like my life had a purpose.

Through that experience, I sought the Lord about what serving Him would look like for me. At the time, the conclusion I heard from Him was to go to Bible college and become a youth pastor so I could do for teenagers what my youth pastor had done for me. With this in mind, I visited my youth pastor's alma mater, Kentucky Christian University. I applied and was accepted. I never visited nor considered another college. Within a matter of weeks, I went from clueless and feeling lost to having a clear purpose and path to make it happen. That was October of my senior year. I spent the rest of the school year stress-free, because I knew where I was going to go to college and what I was going to study. I felt amazing!

As I journeyed through my senior year, I anticipated college more and more. I didn't date much in high school and determined not to worry about it, since I would be heading off to college the following fall. However, God had a different plan.

In February, my youth pastor planned a bus trip to go watch a basketball game between my beloved University of Kentucky Wildcats and our rival University of Tennessee Volunteers. My dad and I signed up to go. When one particular family started to get on the bus, both my youth pastor and senior pastor said to me that, if they were me, they would be hanging out at this family's house getting to know their youngest daughter. I had no clue who they were talking about until (my now-wife) Jill, came on the bus. We spoke a little bit on the bus and the next day I worked up the courage to call her. We didn't know each other at all, so we talked about life and my plans to become a youth pastor. We began a long-distance relationship that lasted over six years. We waited until she graduated from college to get married and start our life together serving in full-time ministry.

For the first 15 years of our marriage, I served as a pastor in three churches. I assumed that would be my life's work until I retired, yet from time to time I felt a discontentment that I couldn't quite explain. I reached the pinnacle of working as an Executive Pastor, the highest level role I desired to have. I started thinking at age 35, *"Am I really going to do this for the next 30 years of my life?"* I determined to stay the course until God directed me otherwise.

But there was a nagging thought in the back of my mind that wouldn't go away. I sometimes wondered what it would look like to make a Kingdom impact in the business community, but this didn't make sense to me. I didn't have a business degree or any business experience outside of churches.

During some very difficult church leadership struggles, I cried out asking God what was next for me. I talked with people from different industries and non-profits to explore what I could do differently as a career. I felt like something was about to change in my life. Leaving full-time ministry felt almost sacrilegious, yet, that's what I felt God leading me to do. It was a very scary and unsettling time.

During that season of searching, I decided to join the John Maxwell Team (JMT) to become a certified leadership coach, speaker and trainer. This would give me ongoing training and support, in case I was supposed to make a career change. That step led me to start a coaching and training business on the side. Less than two months after joining the JMT, things became really scary. I started sensing that God was calling me to step out in faith and leave my *"secure"* church job before I had an established business. I wrestled with that for a few months before surrendering. I started having visions of Abraham being called by God to leave all that was comfortable to him and follow Him to a land where He would show him. (Genesis 12) Abraham was called to blindly follow and trust God. While I wanted that type of faith, I didn't want the scary part of leaving my comfort zone. But God continued to speak to my spirit.

I chose to step out in faith and believed God was going to honor my obedience and open doors for unbelievable success from day one. However, two opportunities that I thought were *"shoe-ins"* for new clients fell through when I had just let go of my full-time salary. We were living on my wife's teaching salary alone now. I was not in a good mental place. I began doubting if I heard God right. I started getting mad at God about why my family was in this situation that we didn't ask for. As I look back, I sounded a lot like the grumbling Israelites in the desert after Moses led them out of slavery in Egypt. Despite being free from a bad situation, I felt like God had led me out into the desert to die. I was in the middle of a spiritual battle and I felt like I was losing!

The pressure was mounting and I started to panic about how to provide financially for my family. I decided to get a part-time job at a hotel, which meant I would be working evenings 3-4 nights a week. I only saw my wife and kids each morning to get them on the bus and out the door. I wouldn't see them again until the next morning. I couldn't be involved with my family's evening activities as usual. While I admire people doing whatever they need to do to provide for their families, I realized this was a decision I made out of fear, not faith, and the job wasn't paying me much for the price I was paying by being away from home.

Three months after beginning this job, my family and I were on vacation. I was studying, praying and asking the Lord what He wanted for me and my family. He kept telling me to trust Him. Right before vacation, He had given us the ability to purchase a home when our lease was up at the house we were renting. This was a miracle since I had no steady income and we were depending on my wife's teaching salary alone. Instead of owing $3,000-$4,000 as we anticipated, we were given a check at closing for over $1,500! The week we were moving into our new home, He provided my wife a new teaching job in a great school district. This was such a lift after she had a miserable teaching experience the year before. Now, God was telling me to quit the hotel job and trust Him. I obeyed. I called my manager while on vacation to give my notice. Once again, I felt free.

Around this time, a good friend pointed me to Steven Furtick's (Elevation Church) sermon called *"Don't Stop on 6."* It was about the story of Joshua leading the Israelites around the city of Jericho. On the seventh day, the army was to march around Jericho seven times, then blow a horn and watch what God would do. One of Furtick's teaching points was that God didn't start chipping away bricks each lap they took. Rather, they had to faithfully march all seven laps and obey God, THEN He destroyed the wall of Jericho all at once and gave them victory. If they would have stopped on lap six or sooner, they wouldn't have experienced victory! Through this message, I was inspired to keep moving forward and keep the faith. God was stretching and building me.

So, what does this have to do with Galatians 5:25?

Over the years, I've kept in step with the Spirit of God unintentionally. I've *"accidentally"* walked the path that God was leading me down. Several years ago, I read Galatians 5:25 with fresh eyes. It leapt off the page at me. I realized that I had been ignoring the Holy Spirit's role in my life. Thankfully, the Spirit had not been ignoring me!

As I read this Scripture over and over, I realized that I often run ahead of God, yet I am called to keep in step with His Spirit day by day. I have a very driven personality that wants to get things done YESTERDAY! I'm action-oriented. I'm known as a *"get-it-done guy."* I have a hard time obeying Psalm 46:10 - *"Be still and know that I am God."* To me, being still feels lazy. I need to get up and make something happen! Yet, keeping in step with the Spirit requires me to dial back my ambition. It requires me to let go of control and seek God's will. It requires me to abide in Christ. It requires me to stop, pray and ask God for my next steps rather than coming up with them on my own.

One fall day in 2016, I was becoming tired of trying to make things happen. I was feeling worn out. I decided to ask the Lord what He wanted me to do rather than trying to figure things out on my own, which wasn't working. I simply asked, *"What do you want me to do today?"* I heard the Spirit say to me *"Go for a run."* PROBLEM - I don't like running! I'm in fairly good physical shape, but I've never enjoyed running. Training for a half-marathon several years ago just about killed me! But I chose to be obedient and went for a run around my neighborhood. Afterwards, nothing seemed different other than feeling more peaceful. The next day, I asked the same question of God and this time I heard the Spirit tell me to *"take a walk."* This was a much better request! However, my reaction was *"But, I should be getting to work. I should be in my office producing something."* Again I obeyed this prompting and went for a walk.

As I was walking, I was asking the Lord why He wanted me to be walking instead of working. I was having an argument with Him in my mind. As I came to the end of my street, I sensed the Spirit telling me to take another lap. I immediately thought, *"You've got to be kidding me!"* But I obeyed. On the second lap, it was as if the Lord was tackling some issues in my life where I lacked trust in Him. One of those issues was about trusting Him to be my family's provider, not me. He was also telling me that my value to my family is more than my financial contribution. I had been wrestling with this for quite some time through this new season of life. He was directly addressing it with me on my walk.

As I was walking lap two, God reminded me what He had been doing over the previous months. As I finished lap two, I felt the Spirit telling me to take another lap. At this point I said, *"Lord, am I going to be walking this neighborhood seven times today?!"* I started wondering how I would answer my wife when she came home and asked what I had done that day. I imagined how embarrassed I would feel if I told her I just walked a lot! My ego was on the line. But I obeyed. God continued to challenge my thinking.

As I finished lap three, I was pleasantly surprised that I didn't feel the prompting to go another lap. Instead, I went home and called my friend Mark. Mark spoke into my life that day telling me that God simply wants to spend time with me and to do that He needed me to get out of my house away from distractions and the temptation to do busy work. It was a powerful revelation to me and I am very grateful for it.

Mark also pointed me to the July 6th reading in My Utmost for His Highest by Oswald Chambers. Chambers wrote that God first gives us a vision, and then He takes us through a valley to batter us into the person we need to become so we can achieve that vision. WOW! That was eye opening. I definitely had been feeling battered over the past 18 months. Now I was starting to understand things from different perspective.

I am still a work in progress. However, I am more mindful that God has great plans for me and I don't have to make them happen on my own. Not only does He love me and have plans for me, He has given me His Spirit to guide, direct and correct me daily.

Keeping in step with the Holy Spirit isn't easy. There are many things that don't make earthly sense when you're following the Spirit, but as followers of Jesus we are called to help build the Kingdom of God.

The Kingdom is built on *"upside down"* principles. One example: The last shall be first and the first shall be last. (Matthew 20:16) Another example: The greatest among you will be the servant of all. (Matthew 23:11) These things don't make sense from an earthly perspective, but through the lens of faith, they make complete sense. God is at work in people who operate by His standards and practices rather than the world's standards.

Take a look at your life.

Where are you out of step with the Spirit?

Where are you trying to make things happen on your own?

Where do you need to surrender and trust God to lead you by His Spirit each day?

When I felt like God was leading me out into the desert to die, I think

I was right. He was leading me to die to myself. He was leading me to a place of true dependence on Him. He was taking me to a place where I can't achieve or succeed on my own strength. While I believe that my family has been faithfully following God for years, we are now experiencing what it means to truly live by faith, not by sight.

While I realize your journey will be different than mine, my prayer is that you will experience the full life of keeping in step with the Spirit of God. When the days seem dark, don't be afraid, have courage, hang on and keep following. God will lead you through difficult seasons to grow and prepare you to achieve the plans for which He has created you. Embrace the journey and praise Him for it along the way!

ABOUT CHRIS MCCLURE

Chris McClure is the Founder and President of Lead Life BIG, a Professional Coaching and Leadership Training company in the Dayton, OH area. He is a certified member of The John Maxwell Team. His mission is to equip individuals, teams and organizations to clarify their purposes and break through barriers so they can reach their potential. For more than 17 years he served as a full-time youth and executive pastor where he led both paid and volunteer staff members. He is very active in his local church and community. He is married to his high school sweetheart, Jill, and they have three children - Ryan, Evan and Anna.

Contact Chris:
- Website: www.LeadLifeBIG.com
- LinkedIn: www.LinkedIn.com/in/ChrisrMcClure
- Facebook: www.Facebook.com/LeadLifeBIG
- Twitter: www.Twitter.com/LeadLifeBIG
- Instagram: www.Instagram.com/LeadLifeBIG
- Email: Chris@LeadLifeBIG.com
- Phone: 770-715-8280

DO THE THING WHICH YOU THINK YOU CANNOT DO

By Garrett Milby

DO THE THING WHICH YOU THINK YOU CANNOT DO

"You gain strength, courage and confidence by every experience in which you really stop to look fear in the face. You must do the thing which you think you cannot do." - Eleanor Roosevelt

Think about this for a moment: fear is crippling, heart stopping, a hindrance, sometimes just a plain nuisance. Fear manifests itself in many different ways through phobias, anxieties, jitters. The fear of public speaking, the fear of germs, the fear of death, the fear of being alone—just search *"fears"* and you can find all of the many fears that can hinder each of us.

Amazingly, sadly, FEAR is the leading cause for keeping so many of us from reaching our true full potential in life.

Fear is and will be the root cause for some of the greatest inventions, businesses, books and more never becoming realities. Why? Simple. Some individuals will never be able to overcome the constant state of fear that strangles them. How does so much fear manifest in the lives of so many people? Is it engrained? Are individuals born with it? That may be one of greatest mysteries of the world never solved. However, the truth is we all have an innate ability to stare fear in the face and overcome those phobias that bind us. If we learn healthy strategies to address the fears that place a stranglehold on our lives, we are actually able to become much more than we realize and become a testament of proof to others that they too can become courageous overcomers.

As a child, young adult and adult, there were numerous things that scared me, leaving me apprehensive:

- I was fearful of heights (acrophobia). I was never afraid to ascend, it was the descend that got me. I remember vividly as a child I climbed on top of our garage with my father while it was being built. It was a proud moment in my life to be about 12 feet off the ground—having a king of the world mentality. It was short lived because what goes up must come down. Needless to say, I insisted that my father needed to call the fire department to come get me off that roof. No fire departments were needed to rescue me that day, only my dad and a bucket loader.

- I was fearful of snakes (ophidiophobia) to the point that if I saw one I would kill it. Then, my compassionate side would take over and I would cry until we gave it a proper burial—because what harm can a dead snake actually cause a person, right?

- After reading the book of Revelation as a young boy (don't recommend), I became fearful of the dark, particularly the walk-in closet in my room. I was overcome with fearful thoughts that the Devil was lurking in my closet, waiting to come out, and pull me into the depths of Hell.

- I was fearful of tight spaces (claustrophobia). I was filled with panic because I was unable to escape in a moment's notice.

- I was fearful of becoming a husband; unsure I could provide for my wife properly.

- I was fearful of becoming a father; uncertain I could become the selfless individual fatherhood requires.

In hindsight and through reflection, maybe I was fearful of fear (phobophobia).

I am sure that, if you are like me, several of the fears that I listed above might resonate with you. Some fears are only temporary, some fears are lifelong hindrances and some fears we have the opportunity to overcome—possibly getting to the point where we can look back and laugh at them because of how silly those fears might have been.

Of all the fears that keep one from reaching full potential, public speaking (glossophobia), fear of failure (atychiphobia) and fear of what others thought of me, were probably the ones that crippled me most. However, through personal, physical and spiritual growth, I was able to grasp those fears and conquer them. For you to truly understand my overcoming courageous story, you need to understand how I was able to combat and conquer my fears.

Have you ever been in a situation that did not really make sense at the time, but later on in life you were able to make sense of it? Of course you have, we all have. That is exactly what happened to me. Having been raised in a Christian home all of my life, I have been taught over and over what things are good and what things are bad. Being truthful and transparent, I must admit I am a child of divorced parents. While divorce is often seen as a negative, I have tried to see the silver lining from such an event and so began my journey from fear to find courage.

At the age of ten, my father introduced me to my future step mother (fearful). While I was apprehensive to add another female figure into my life, God's plan was bigger than my own. My father and stepmother would wed a few short months later and the journey began as a blended family. There was my dad, my sister and I, and my stepmother and her two daughters. As you could imagine, blending a family of future teenagers is not as easy as the Brady Bunch made it out to be. However, this was all part of God's plan. My stepmother would end up being very influential in my spiritual journey.

As a young boy at about age eleven, I started a journey that I simply call *"The Race"*. It was a race I started to run, even though running of the physical nature is not in my DNA. I started running a spiritual race that had numerous detours along the way. God had called me to run the race for Him, and I knew it from a young age. I just did not know what type of calling He had placed upon my life.

I can still remember my family inviting our pastor to our house. I was so impressed with him that I wanted to be like him. For that one dinner, I dressed up like, you guessed it, a pastor. I found one of my dad's old suits and put it on. It was a grey pin-striped three-piece suit. I buttoned my white collar shirt up and put on a necktie. I really thought I was something. I placed my pocket-sized Gideon Bible in the left breast pocket of my jacket because every pastor needs his Bible with him. I was as proud as a peacock, strutting around the house waiting for our pastor and his family to arrive. When they did, I got the instant affirmation I was looking for when he told me *"I looked like a preacher."* Of course, at that young age, I never really thought about being a preacher—I just wanted to play one. Little did I know, this was foreshadowing to what my life would become.

Several years passed by and the idea of becoming a preacher became a distant memory. But, God never stopped working on me. There were often times in prayer that I would pray for God to reveal himself to me, which He did, and of course I would shy away from such grand commitments to into servanthood for God. As my stepmother continued to pour into my life and my walk with God grew, I could see how God could eventually use me, if I was willing.

I have always had an outgoing personality, have never met a stranger, and have always had a compassionate heart for others. However, none of that mattered. At the age of 14, I truly started to believe that God was calling me to be His servant. This is when I experienced my first detour.

One night after the sermon at one of our church's revivals, the pastor asked if anyone had a testimony they would like to share. As the Spirit was pouring into me, I could no longer hold back. I gathered every ounce of courage that I could, I stood up, and I gave a testimony for the first time. Remember, I said earlier that public speaking is a fear of mine. On that night, fear could not contain me. I had something to say, and I was going to say it.

On the second night of revival, I felt called to say something again. Here I was this fourteen year old boy standing up amongst giants speaking again. The ending of this night would not go as planned.

You see, often times we become rather prideful and often times there are people among us who are willing to bring us back down to reality. That night, my father stepped in and crushed my spirit. While we all traveled home from revival in our Chevy Astro van, I learned a harsh lesson. Pride got the best of me. I committed *"the cardinal sin"* when I asked my father what he thought about me giving my testimony. My father answered with these words which forever cut through me to my core: *"Garrett, just because you have something to say does not mean you always have to say it."*

There I was a fourteen year old young man *"on fire"* for God and his words took the wind right out of my sails. It was at that moment, while I was obviously overly prideful, his words were the straw that broke this camel's back. I went from being a Spirit-filled, *"on fire"*, young man seeking God's own heart to a humbled, embarrassed, ashamed teenager with a broken spirit. While my father was only offering his wisdom and guidance to me, little did he know that he actually killed any desire to speak for God again, any desire to stand in front of a crowd, and any desire to deliver my testimony. I became bounded by heavy chains—chains that would bind me for years to come.

Now, I will not say that those words were the reason for what happened next in my life, leading me down a path of minimal destruction, but that moment changed the trajectory of my life for that season. After that moment, I was filled with fear. I swore to never speak again. I started to allow what others thought of me or might think of me to deter me from any possibility of serving God.

From the age of 14-18, one would say I made several *"questionable at best"* decisions during such a critical time in life. I always carried a macho persona on the outside, looking like I was well put together. On the outside, you saw a popular individual—a person who was heavily involved with the football team, had numerous friends, belonged to several school clubs, etc. But, on the inside I was a mess.

What happens when we are mess? Often, we try to seek our identity in temporary fulfillment in this world. That is exactly what I did. I turned to things of this world. I became a part of this world. While I never got too far gone, I became rebellious to my parent's rules. I filled my life with things like alcohol, failed relationships and burdensome friendships. I turned my back on God, but He never once turned His back on me.

Unfortunately, I was running a race that could not be won without Him. With all that was going wrong, I did the best thing I thought I could do: I ran.

In August of 2001, I reported for Navy boot camp in Great Lakes. I thought leaving everything behind and creating a new life would help me reclaim my life and purpose. Unfortunately, no matter how far I ran, I could not out run problems or God. While in boot camp things did not get any better, I became depressed and wanted out of the military.

After completing boot camp, I can remember praying to God: *"If you will provide for me away to get out of here, I promise I will serve you the rest of my life, only if it is your will."*

Fast-forwarding a few months into December 2001, I was notified that I was being sent home. I was out of the military thanks to a technicality that I found on my enlistment. Talk about a loophole saving a person! By February 2002 I was finally back home. Praise the Lord for answered prayers! It was now time to get my life back on track, so I thought.

What does a man do when granted new opportunities? Upon returning home, things did not change for me. I still remained an uncertain young man seeking purpose in life. I moved in with my grandparents and started a job. Things were looking up. However, I still could not find peace in the choices I had made.

I remembered the prayer I prayed to God, but I was not willing to give Him all of me just yet. So what did I do, I bartered with God. I became a great barterer. I remember my conversations with God vividly. They went a little something like this: God, if you will…

- allow me to have a good job (He has provided for me and my family for years now),

- provide me with a future wife (He gave me a beautiful wife, who believed in me and encouraged me. We will celebrate 14 years together this May, nine years of marriage),

- allow me to go to college and graduate (He allowed me to

obtain a Master's degree),

- provide me with a family of my own (He gave two beautiful children: a son and a daughter)...

I WILL FOLLOW YOU!

The craziest of things happened: God provided everything to me and I gave nothing more to Him in return than what was required. But, God will only allow these actions to go on for so long. A moment will come where you will either give yourself to Him or you will feel the emptiness of no pursuit. So what happened?

Ten years later I finally surrendered to God's calling on my life. Finally at the age of 28 years old; I surrendered all, not knowing what the call might be. After 14 years of running, I made a decision to start following God, whatever it might mean, wherever it might be.

Finally in February of 2011, I met with my pastor to discuss what had been laid on my heart. In that moment, my pastor let me know that God had shared with him I was being called into His service, but he did not want to force the issue. I had been battling God for years clawing, scratching, dismissing God, and finally I cautiously laid down my sword and stopped the battle. I say cautiously, because I had no idea what God was calling me to do.

A few months went by and my pastor let me know that he wanted to give me an opportunity to share my testimony when I was ready. I reluctantly said, *"Yes."* Yet, fear was still holding me back.

I had reenlisted in the Navy in 2004 because I felt I had let my country down. I was scheduled to give my testimony in September

2011. However, an engine blew on the airplane I was flying on with the military which delayed my return home. I dodged a bullet there. No speaking for me. I was not prepared to surrender to God's calling yet and this was my excuse to get out of it.

Why was I so fearful? I knew this was God's timing and plan. Here's why, I still lacked confidence in myself. Who am I? I often thought. I continued to remember the words of my father from years earlier. I worried what others would think of me. How would my decision affect my family if I announced the call to ministry? What about all of my past failures and indiscretions—would they come back to haunt me? What if I failed? All of those questions of self-doubt continued to pop into my head.

Finally, it happened. One morning while driving down the interstate, God spoke to me. He said, *"The time is now! You have run long enough, my child! I have given you all of Me and it is time for you to give Me all of you!"*

In that moment, what does a person do? I broke down in tears. I had finally come to the conclusion that God was right, I was wrong to foolishly battle with Him. I will be the first to admit that God had given me everything I ever wanted and I had only given Him a minimal effort at best.

It was in that moment that the fear of speaking, the fear of what others thought of me, the fear of being a failure no longer mattered and I was at peace knowing God had already prepared me for everything that was going to happen. It was in that moment that I stopped fighting fear and found the courage to become what God intended me to be when He created me in the womb.

It was in that moment that I laid down my life to become a servant-leader for others. It was in that moment that fear no longer had dominion over me and that God's power would be enough to take me all the way to my journey's end. It was in that moment that I finally felt like I had found a sense of purpose, life had meaning and that none of the blessings I have received would have been made possible without overcoming fear. I now know COURAGE—WITH GOD, ALL THINGS ARE POSSIBLE!

ABOUT GARRETT MILBY

Garrett W. Milby is native Kentuckiana who has a heart for serving others, assisting them with matters of the heart, motivating and empowering them to rise above their current situations and brining about a clearer vision for tomorrow. However, none of this would have been made possible, if it was not for Garrett having the courage to overcome his own fears, and seeing the plan God had for his own life.

Garrett is a lifelong learner of leadership, having graduated from college with a BS in Workforce Leadership and Development and a MA in Organizational Leadership. In 2015, Garrett became a Certified Speaker, Coach and Trainer under the hand of the #1 Leadership Guru in the World John C. Maxwell.

Garrett is a published author of Born to L.E.A.D: Leveraging Efforts and Attitudes into Dreams. Additionally, Garrett is a seasoned Admissions Representative working with students throughout Kentucky, assisting students and families in selecting proper college and career pathways. Garrett has spent the last 13 years serving with the Kentucky Air National Guard achieving the rank of Master Sergeant. In his spare time you can find him enjoying landscaping and spending time with his family. Garrett contributes all his blessings to the grace of God.

Contact Garrett
- Website: www.MilbyEnterprises.com
- LinkedIn: www.LinkedIn.com/in/Garrett-Milby-34779960
- Facebook: www.Facebook.com/Garrett.Milby
- Email: MilbyEnterprises@outlook.com
- Phone: 502-931-2679

THE MAKING OF A WARRIOR

By Edward Reed

THE MAKING OF A WARRIOR

Growing up, I was blessed to have a loving mom and dad along with four brothers—three younger and one older. As a child, I never understood that courage is taking action to fight fear on the battlefield. Over the years, I've learned to fight for my beliefs, despite my fears, using the resources and gifts God has given me to overcome the barriers to fulfilling my purpose.

Elementary school was a rough time of life; I hated it. I was often teased, felt lonely, had low self-esteem, felt disconnected and only had a few friends. There were times when I got into fights with kids and even got jumped by a couple of them. I will never forget that day when Eddie and Dereck held me on the blacktop, punching and kicking me. I didn't fight back. I just laid there frozen. Others watched without helping me. I felt no one cared.

One of my worst days was the day my elementary school teacher called all the students together for an announcement. While we all sat on the floor, she said, *"Edward Reed and Beth..., you two are being moved to the small class."* It was the class other kids called the class for *"dummies"* where no one wanted to be. It was hard enough being bullied for just being me. Hearing this, I ran to the back of the room and cried.

Imagine what could have happened, if just one adult would have talked to me about my performance instead of moving me to the small class. Imagine someone speaking the words: *"You seem sad. I know you can do better. How can I help you?"* Yet, I simply didn't understand why people would bother me. I just wished they would leave me alone. My attitude toward school slowly changed as I went through the motions.

One day everything came crashing down. I decided I didn't want to live any longer. I snuck into my room with a bottle of pills from the medicine cabinet, and took the whole bottle. Somehow my brothers found out, told my mom and things got crazy. Mom was so worried. I loved her so much. My older brother rushed me to the hospital. I hated life and the pain I was going through. My parents didn't know how I felt inside. In the hospital, my stomach was pumped for several hours. We returned home and I realized how worried my parents had become. While talking with my aunt, she told me how much I was loved, especially by my parents.

In secondary school, my mindset had changed. Getting a little tougher, I gravitated toward tougher kids. My fear of being bullied led me to friends who didn't get bullied. I didn't value school.

One spring day in eighth grade, my school counselor called me to his office to discuss my classes. He began, *"I've been reviewing your test scores and you shouldn't be in the small classes. Do you think you can handle the regular English class?"* With a little attitude, I courageously replied, *"Of course, I can."* I was moved to the regular class. He planted word seeds of transformation by opening a door of opportunity for me. I actually earned a *"B"* in the course. The rest of my grades were pretty low. My grades were a reflection of my attitude—not my ability.

In high school, I discovered the wrong antidote to fear: sex, drugs and alcohol. School for me was about hanging out and making new friends. No longer the sad kid from elementary school, I just didn't care anymore and it showed in my academic performance.

I spent two years in a reading class with two other students. Our teacher Mrs. Thornton was phenomenal; I didn't mind. My parents had a fit every nine weeks when they saw my report card. I got punished for nine weeks each time. Since they worked so much, I just snuck around and did my thing.

The last marking period of 9th grade, I brought my grades up so I could play football. Sophomore year, I made the JV Football team and thought I was cool. Unfortunately, I put little stock in academics and became ineligible to play in my junior year.

I discovered skipping school and friends with cars. On weekends, I went to clubs, pretending to be older than reality. Back then, if you blended with the crowd, no one checked your ID. My grades were just good enough to pass.

By the end of junior year, I was eligible to play sports. I had been looking forward to playing football my senior year. After working out, pulling my grades up and tryouts, I made the varsity team.

Right before the first game, I told my mother I was playing football. She asked, *"Who gave you permission to play football? You are not playing football. Your grades were terrible when you played. You are going to college!"* I replied, *"I am not going to college."* My mom was no joke and she's still no joke. I turned in my equipment alright and stayed mad from September to March.

A marine recruiter phoned one day and said, *"Look here boy, you know you aint going to get into nobody's college. So why don't you just get on the bus and come on down here and sign up."* I responded, *"I aint your boy. I can go to college."*

The next day, I went to my school counselor Mr. Howard and asked: *"What do I have to do to go to college?"* With a friendly smile, he replied by shaking his head side to side, *"Eddie, let's pretend you had a 2.0 GPA (my cumulative GPA was 1.98) and you get an average score on the SAT. You can get into some state schools."*

Mr. Howard printed a list of schools to apply to and helped me register for the SAT. My parents enrolled me into an SAT prep class. Though my scores were low, I applied to Bowie State and they risked accepting me based on my potential, not for my transcript scores. In my freshmen year, Bowie State provided me an opportunity and resources to transform my perspective on life.

Dr. Clemmie Solomon took me under wing along with 25 other young men. We needed fresh perspective. He gathered us together in the evening during freshmen orientation to talk with us about life. Extremely intentional about leading us through a transformation process, he was my number one mentor, often speaking life into me throughout my college career and beyond. Dr. Solomon believed in me more than I believed in myself.

At Bowie, I got to know and experience the love of God through Jesus Christ. Don't get me wrong, I was not a saint. As a kid, I went to church. But, I never really knew Jesus.

In January 1989, fear barged back into my life through my poor decision making. As an immature 19 year old, I thought guys were supposed to be *"players"*. We told young ladies what we thought they wanted to hear to attract them.

One night drunk at a party, I met a young lady. We danced all night. I told her all kinds of sweet things about us being together. For weeks, we talked on the phone until one of my buddies told me she was bad news. She didn't attend Bowie, but she came to our campus parties. Little did I realize, I made her feel so special she got attached to the idea of us *"becoming a couple"*. I cut her off without conversation.

A friend from her neighborhood told me she was trying to find someone to shoot me. Far from being the wimpy elementary kid, in my mind I was fearless. I had seen all kinds of things from hanging out in the city, but I could not shake this fear. I was loving life and scared of losing it, and I didn't want to be bothered with her.

After weeks of invitations, I agreed to go to a Bible study with a friend. Pastor Branson shared God's Word about the importance of making a difference. I realized it was time to step up. I accepted Jesus as my Savior that night. After Bible study, I apologized to the young lady for misleading her and hurting her feelings. We worked things out. I had become a new person in my Savior, Jesus Christ. My thinking and my life were transformed by the Word.

College was a great experience. My grades improved. Intentionally, I sought to add value to others through community service projects and by serving in various leadership roles. As a result, I was honored with various awards and recognitions.

Coached by my parents, and mentored by Dr. Solomon and a team of loving people, I worked in private industry as a project manager for a transportation company. This company held federal contracts to provide shuttle bus services for various government agencies. My responsibility was to supervise a team of shuttle bus drivers (who were mostly 20 years older than me) and to repair damage between the company and a government contracting officer. I was asked to use my gift in relationship management to save the contract.

Intrigued by human behavior, I went to graduate school to study counseling psychology with a goal to gain insight into human behavior. Dr. Solomon convinced me to change my major from counseling psychology to school counseling, even though I had no intention of becoming a school counselor after graduation. I saw myself as a business man ready to join another company serving as an operations manager overseeing company contracts providing security services for government agencies. I had a proven track record of successfully managing government contracts, leading people and building relationships with key players.

The company president asked me to cut the hours of all full-time employees to part-time to save money on health insurance. I opposed his decision, explaining the impact that low morale from his seeming disloyalty would have on his bottom line. In light of our disagreement, I resigned from his company.

Networking with friends and family, I started working in business development with PageNet. New technology entered the marketplace and loyalty to unproductive partnerships blocked capitalization on new opportunities. It was time for me to exit since the writing was on the wall. The problem was *those on the inside didn't read the walls from the outside"*. Market dominance was suddenly about to shift.

I went to work as a UPS sales representative in the business development division. This was one of the best work experiences in my life (not for the income but) for what I learned as I visited clients and built new business.

Another life changing moment happened one day after I had just left The Coca-Cola Company's government affairs office on Connecticut Ave in Washington, DC. Coca-Cola was one of several accounts I managed for UPS. As I walked down the street, a husband and wife were sitting on the sidewalk holding a cardboard sign and a cup asking for help. I walked right passed them, then heard a female voice yell, *"Hey brother, you in that fine suit, do you think you are too good to help somebody?"* Feeling convicted, I walked back and put some money in their cup.

The following day, I walked past the same gentleman sitting in the same spot. This time he was reading. Standing over him, I asked,

"What are you reading?" He replied, *"The Bible."* I asked, *"What do you know about that?"* He answered, *"I'm just trying to make peace with my life. I have HIV, lost my job with all my doctor appointments, lost my house, gave the disease to my wife, have a son in middle school and we live in a family shelter."* Sarcastically, I said, *"How did you get HIV?"* He responded, *"Bad blood. I got a blood transfusion from DC General Hospital in southeast DC."* Once he mentioned DC General, I felt lower than I have ever felt in my life. Growing up in Silver Spring, MD, I knew never to go to DC General.

After this encounter, I walked and talked with God about His desires for my life. I asked Him, *"How would this man's life have been different if he would have had the same kind of people in his life that I had in mine? If he would have had someone to guide him as a young teen, would he have been in this situation?"* The question that always advances my journey came to me, *"God, what would You have me to do?"* After a short time at UPS, the message became crystal clear: God gifted me to work with young people and families. Until that very point, I was being trained through personal life experiences and formal education to make a difference in the lives of others.

I was not crazy about God's answer. Yes, I tried to negotiate. I said, *"Let's wait about 20 years and let me make some money."* Less than enthusiastically, I began to reach out to people I knew from the years I had earned my degree in Counseling. Surprisingly, nobody returned my calls. I said, *"Oh well, maybe I'm wrong."* At the same time, as a salesman, I always kept my options open for a BBD (bigger better deal).

I learned about a tech company looking for account managers to work with clients to grow their professional development training business in greater Washington DC. This was a perfect fit for me: I had sales experience, specialized in relationship management and had a Master's Degree in Education. The average account manager was making 100K. Perhaps, God was good with my waiting 20 years. I interviewed and made first cut.

I then received a phone call from Jane Woodburn, a human resource specialist with Montgomery County Public Schools asking if I was interested in a long-term school counseling substitute position. *"Are there any benefits?"* I asked. She replied, *"No, let me ask you a question. Why would you have a degree to work with students and not be using it? Are you happy doing what you are doing right now?"* I answered, *"No, but the money is good."* She responded, *"Would you be willing to just visit Wootton High School and meet the principal to see what you think?"*

I went, met Principal Dr. Becky Newman, and was eventually offered the position. Touring the school with Dr. Newman, my spirit was at peace and I knew this was where I was supposed to be for the next phase of my journey.

On that same evening I was offered the counseling position, I was also invited to a second interview with the tech company. I thought about the difference between $109 per day and $100K per year. I thought about the difference between obedience and disobedience to God's calling. I declined the interview to move forward and shared what I believed was true: *"I've been given an opportunity of a lifetime."*

I developed a friendship with a special education teacher while working as a counselor at the school. Our friendship grew and we both knew there was something more going on between us. Years later, we married and now have two wonderful children.

I had no idea I would return to school to earn another master's degree in School Administration and become a high school assistant principal. After spending 9.5 years in school administration, I asked God in January 2012, *"What would you have me to do with my life?*

How can I best serve you?" Yes, I asked the question, but I was not ready to hear the answer.

God led me to Johns Hopkins School of Education (JHU) to pursue an advanced post master's degree in Counseling and Clinical Supervision. I fussed, *"How can I get my application and recommendation submitted within 30 days?"* God didn't give me advanced notice, nor did I ask my question in advance. My paperwork was submitted before the deadline and I received an invitation to interview for the program.

All set and ready to go, I arrived to the interview 30 minutes late after fighting Baltimore street repairs. The interview went great. When asked why I was applying to the program, I replied, *"God has instructed me to do so and I'm learning how important it is to be obedient to His instructions."*

At the time, I thought I was preparing to build a private counseling practice and phase out of the public school system. When taking the leap of faith to apply to JHU, my plan was to continue working as an assistant principal, complete the program, setup a private practice and become a middle school principal.

A month later, my son called me at work around 9:30 PM crying. I asked, *"Daniel, what is wrong?"* He replied, *"Daddy, I miss you. When are you coming home?"* My heart melted and the lyrics of a popular song played through my head. Once again, I asked God, *"What should I do? Are you using my kids to get to me?"*

I entered a period of fasting and prayer and I sought out my cousin's counsel as a strong man of God and minister. We talked about knowing when God is speaking to you and the confirmations that accompany His instructions. The answer was clear. It was time for me to leave administration. Early one morning, I shared with Rita (our principal's secretary who was a close friend and godly woman) what was happening with me. She encouraged me to enter the ministry. I explained that God would use me in a different way.

I prayed while on the fence, attempting again to negotiate with Him: *"Okay God, I will return to counseling, if Mary Lou retires."* God responded, *"Edward, who do you think you are? If I tell you to do something that is what you need to do. You are not in a position to negotiate with me."* I've learned the closer I get to God, the more direct He is in holding me accountable. Our conversation ended with, *"Yes Lord. I will do what I know I should."*

I simply called Rita saying: *"Go ahead and put me on Joan's calendar. I am moving forward."* Rita replied, *"Ed, you aren't going to believe this, Mary Lou just came in to retire."* What else could I say: *"Rita, you aren't going to believe this, but I told God if Mary Lou retires then I would step down. God then asked me, 'Edward, who do you think you are negotiating with Me?'"* Rita and I praised God together because we both knew He was in every part of our work.

Additional confirmations continued. A person of high rank in the school system encouraged me to apply for a middle school principal position that would have been a great fit for my skill set. My response: *"Thank you so much for thinking of me. This is not the right season for me."* Later, I explained to the person who encouraged me to apply for the position that *"After careful prayer and fasting, I need to move in a different direction."*

On the same evening I was approached, I received my final confirmation from a friend who was a former college provost. We discussed my situation and she shared her story with me about stepping out on faith and being obedient to God's calling for her life.

Within a few weeks, another door opened to lead a school counseling department. This worked out perfectly. I completed my studies at JHU, graduated with a perfect 4.0 GPA, and was inducted into an international professional counseling honors society. I met wonderful people and develop new friendships and used all I learned to impact the lives of students, families and staff members.

Ready to set up a private counseling practice, a series of pitches came across my plate, including a request to provide academic coaching and college planning to the son of a friend. This led to the start of Academic Management Group, LLC formed to help students maximize their potential and position themselves for better options upon graduation. This led to my decision to join the John Maxwell Team where I've learned to add value to people and organizations through leadership coaching, training and keynote speaking.

Membership in the John Maxwell Team has been an amazing experience—full of new insight, wisdom and friendships worldwide. Investing time with like-minded leaders committed to God and service, I see with absolute clarity God's plan for the rest of my life to use my time, talent and treasure is to show Jesus' love as I share the gospel throughout the world while loving God, others and myself.

In the first half of my life, God taught me to trust Him and apply His Word to everything I do. Words spoken to Joshua are relevant today: *"Have I not commanded you? Be strong and courageous. Do not be afraid; do not be discouraged, for the Lord your God will be with you wherever you go."* (Joshua 1:9)

We often find ourselves most fearful in the midst of the storms of life. In those moments, I think about fearful disciples in a boat surrounded by a storm, terrified when they saw Jesus walking on water towards them. Jesus told them, *"Do not be afraid. Take courage.*

I am here." (Matthew 14:27)

A lifetime of preparation has led me to join with another warrior, Tricia Andreassen. While getting to know each other, we discovered God has given us the same vision to *"transform one million lives"*!

Today, my strength is rooted in my faith. This strength gives me the courage to overcome my fear. As a result, I am a warrior dedicated to equipping, encouraging and empowering people of all ages to overcome their fears with the courage and freedom to live a purposeful life. The true treasure of life for me is spending eternity with God, something money cannot buy. I am looking forward to hearing God say, *"Well done, my good and faithful servant!"*

ABOUT EDWARD REED

Ed Reed is a humble leader, who overcame challenges, setbacks and other barriers. Ed credits his success to his faith, parents, professors, mentors and coaches for equipping him with the skills and mindset necessary for beating the odds of attaining success.

Ed is the Founder and CEO of Academic Management Group, LLC – a small business providing coaching, strategic educational and career planning, consulting, personality and career interest assessments and leadership development training services. He currently serves on various advisory boards for nonprofit organizations including the 2016 - 2017 President of the Maryland School Counselor Association. Ed also serves his community by leading the School Counseling department for his local middle school. He has served in various leadership roles in private industry and in secondary schools that have been recognized as among the top 100 schools in America and top 6 secondary schools in Maryland.

Ed is a certified John C. Maxwell International Executive Coach, Leadership Trainer and Keynote Speaker. He is living a life of significance by adding value to others.

Contact Edward:
- Website: www.AcademicManagementGroup.com
- Website: www.JohnMaxwellgroup.com/EdwardReed
- Facebook: www.Facebook.com/AcademicManagementGroupLLC
- Twitter: www.Twitter.com/EReedSpeaks
- Email: EReed@AcademicManagementGroup.com
- Phone: 301-335-6689

LYNDA'S LESSONS
By Karen White

LYNDA'S LESSONS

I went to the best *"pre-cremation celebration"* I've ever attended, after my friend Lynda went Home after her nearly 3-year battle with ovarian cancer. To be honest, it's the only *"pre-cremation"* celebration I've ever attended, but I don't know that any memorial service of any kind I've ever attended so perfectly captured the spirit of the departed as this did. There were tears, and there was palpable evidence of how much she will be missed and how much she is loved, but there was something else that permeated every aspect of the gathering: Hope. As the attendees listened to one of Lynda's favorite songs (*Uptown Funk*) being played and obeyed her instructions *"to dance along to the song"*, I was struck by what great lessons in hope my dear friend had taught me over her journey.

I will never forget the look on Lynda's face nearly 3 years earlier as the hospitalist told her that the next step in her care was to get her set up for *"palliative care"* for her ovarian cancer. What that hospitalist apparently didn't know was that, although Lynda had been in the hospital for a couple of days and had undergone some diagnostic tests, nobody had yet told her that ovarian cancer had been diagnosed. What he also didn't know was that Lynda had been with her sister throughout the *"palliative care"* that was brought in at the end of her sister's tough battle with cancer.

The fear and shock that registered in Lynda's eyes and on her husband's face spurred me into action. As a cancer survivor myself, I knew that *"palliative care"* had more than one meaning, and I also knew a great oncologist who would help explain the diagnosis, treatment and options to Lynda and her family. After the somewhat shell-shocked hospitalist left the room with my request to please get my oncologist on the phone to consult on this case, I turned to my friend and her husband and I was dismayed by what I sensed: fear of and a resignation to the diagnosis. I remember telling Lynda that a diagnosis is simply that, a diagnosis. It isn't the end of the story and it isn't a decree about anything. I firmly believed then, and still believe now, that only God determines the ending to the story and we do not have to be defined by any diagnosis unless we choose to be.

Over the next several months, Lynda went through the course of treatment common for ovarian cancer patients, including chemotherapy. She modified her diet, and it appeared to me that she began to feast on Hope. I remember sitting with her, another dear friend and Lynda's husband the first day of her chemotherapy treatment. It was obviously unknown what the chemotherapy would cause as far as side effects. She knew that she would lose her hair, and likely have side effects including fatigue and increased vulnerability to disease, but a discussion of the potential side effects is only part of the preparation for cancer treatment. That first day of chemotherapy I saw something very different in Lynda's eyes than I had seen in the hospital just a short time before. Instead of fear of the unknown (and known) side effects of the treatment, I saw *hope*, I saw *courage* and I saw a strong *resolve* to go through the treatment with an understanding that she would come out on the other side a victor over the disease. She would tell us: *"I'm a fighter, I'm going to fight this cancer"*! And I, for one, believed her!

What is *HOPE*, anyway? Dictionary.com defines *hope* as *"the feeling that what is wanted can be had or that events will turn out for the best"* and *"to look forward to with desire and reasonable confidence."* I think you could sum up the modern approach to *"hope"* as wishing for something, without any certainty of the outcome and that would be an acceptable approach to the discussion of what hope is. When I think of this kind of hope, I think of someone saying *"I hope it doesn't rain today."*

However, that type of hope is not the *Hope* that I witnessed during

Lynda's journey with cancer that was so appropriately celebrated at her *"pre-cremation"* service, and replaced the fear that many experience during such a journey. The type of Hope that Lynda lived was so much deeper than that, and it is the thing that can sustain us all throughout this journey we call life! What looked to many like simple *"courage"*, I believe was actually the outward expression of Hope.

I believe that COURAGE is impossible without HOPE, and therefore understanding HOPE is necessary if we want to live COURAGEOUS lives.

I describe the kind of *Hope* that I witnessed develop so strongly in my dear friend as an understanding that there is more to come that I can't currently see, and it is grounded in two very important elements: 1) an understanding of who God is and what His promises are, and 2) trust. These two elements are key to moving from a place of fear and uncertainty to a place of courage and action in the face of fear.

Lynda demonstrated this understanding as she completed her chemotherapy. I remember many conversations with her about what was to come...not in her treatment, but after her treatment was complete. She was looking forward to getting back to work, spending time with her family and focusing on the things that were truly important. I remember thinking that she was different than just *"positive"*. It was so much deeper than that, and it really did ooze out of her to splash on the people around her.

Lynda completed her treatment, resumed her work schedule and led a life marked by gratefulness and positivity. It came as a shock to all of us when, nearly two years after her treatment was complete, she began to have disturbing symptoms which led to the discovery that her cancer was back, and with a vengeance not uncommon in recurrent cancer. I'm sure that Lynda had tough moments after the cancer was discovered again, but what impressed me most about her during this time was her unfailing faith and her contagious hope. She endured many difficulties during the next several months, but her text messages to me always included a reminder to me of the goodness of God and her unwavering knowledge that God was firmly in control.

At her *"pre-cremation"* service, her husband and I had a discussion about how Lynda had become so strong in her faith as a result of her disease and treatment. Her approach to her situation was the opposite of others I've know who have received unexpected diagnoses, faced serious health issues and have chosen to question or be angry at God for their situation or to dive deep into the pit of fear and uncertainty in response to the unknown. Lynda took refuge in God's promises which transformed her.

What are some of God's promises that can lead us to be grounded in an understanding of who He is, and can help us combat fear with faith, courage and hope?

Here are some of my favorites:

2 Corinthians 1:3-4 (NIV) *"Praise be to the God and Father of our Lord Jesus Christ, the Father of compassion and the God of all comfort, who comforts us in all our troubles, so that we can comfort those in any trouble with the comfort we ourselves receive from God."*

Psalm 107:13-16 (NIV) *"Then they cried out to the Lord in their trouble, and he saved them from their distress. He brought them out of darkness, the utter darkness and broke away their chains. Let them give thanks to the Lord for his unfailing love and his wonderful deeds for mankind, for he breaks down gates of bronze and cuts through bars of iron."*

Joshua 1:9 (NIV) *"Have I not commanded you? Be strong and courageous. Do not be afraid; do not be discouraged, for the Lord your God will be with you wherever you go."*

John 14:27 (NIV) *"Peace I leave with you, my peace I give you. I do not give to you as the world gives. Do not let your hearts be troubled and do not be afraid."*

Jeremiah 29:11-13 (NIV) *"For I know the plans I have for you, declares the Lord, plans to prosper you and not to harm you, plans to give you hope and future. Then you will call on me and come and pray to me, and I will listen to you. You will seek me and find me when you seek me with all your heart."*

Ephesians 3:20-21 (NIV) *"Now to him who is able to do immeasurably more than all we ask or imagine, according to his power that is at work within us, to him be glory in the church and in Christ Jesus throughout all generations, for ever and ever! Amen."*

In addition to understanding who God is and what He says He'll do, Hope inspired courage requires TRUST. Trust is the firm belief in the reliability, truth, ability or strength of something or someone. It is possible to understand something, but not believe in the reliability of that same thing. That is why trust is the second requisite to Hope. Trust takes the knowledge that God can and turns it into belief that He will, which is the foundation of Hope, and shows up in our lives in the form of courage.

Lynda went home far too soon, and she will be forever missed by her family and friends. But Lynda left a legacy that not everyone takes the opportunity to build: she inspired people, and she changed the lives of those who met her and learned of her story, yet witnessed this unmistakable hope that marked her and radiated from her.

What lessons did Lynda teach me throughout her journey? I've come up with ten *"truths"* that I witnessed and learned from my dear, sweet friend. I've named them *"Lynda's Lessons."*

1. Hope is so much more than *"wishing."* I never once heard Lynda say, *"I wish that hadn't happened,"* or *"I wish I didn't have to go through this,"* or *"I wish this was over."* I don't know whether she consciously decided to avoid these phrases, or whether the absence of these phrases stemmed from the fact that she didn't actually have those thoughts. Nevertheless, the result was that her unwavering stance was that she had Hope in and from God. After her cancer returned and her symptoms worsened, her thoughts were to those who would be left behind, and her message to them was clear, and powerful...don't stay stuck in the grief of the moment, life is precious and life is to be lived. Lynda certainly embodied an attitude that *"even if it rains, life will be ok and you'll come out of it better than you can imagine."*

2. Hope is a verb—active and involved. The kind of hope that is limited to *"I hope it doesn't rain"* is very passive...relying on something that may or may not happen. The kind of Hope Lynda embodied was an active hope, the intentional belief and reliance on the goodness of God's love that can and does transform lives.

3. Hope is always bigger than your circumstances. One of the things that I loved most about Lynda was her future focus, which I believe was a byproduct of her Hope. She was not focused only on herself, her treatment or her next step (although I know she considered those things). She was focused on how her situation would and could influence others. I believe that's why she asked us all to dance to *Uptown Funk* at her memorial...it is very hard not to smile

when you are remembering with fondness someone's zest for life embodied in a song played at top volume as she rode down the street! That promise of brighter days and joy is what makes Hope so profound...even though my situation may seem dark and difficult...Hope takes me to a place where joy and beauty remain.

4. Hope knows that God promises that He has a plan and that plan is not for harm. I have heard people who have received a troubling diagnosis or difficult news ask *"Why would God do this to me?"* Hope knows that God does not give us trouble, or cause us pain...Hope knows that God loves us and has a plan that we can't even begin to wrap our minds around. Ephesians 3:20-21 (NIV) reminds us that God is able to do immeasurably more than all we ask or imagine, according to his power that is at work within us. I find great comfort in knowing that God is so much bigger than I can even begin to wrap my mind around. Hope trusts that even when we can't see the whole picture and we can't, in the moment, understand what the plan could be, that there is a plan and that plan is for good and not harm.

5. Hope always wins. Even though Lynda left us far too early for my liking, Lynda lived more than some people I've met who have exceeded her lifespan in years. Because Lynda had Hope, her days were full with love and joy...and I think that that's a win in the *"good life"* category.

6. Hope is contagious. It was impossible to be around Lynda and be down! She simply wouldn't hear of it, and seeing her in the hallway at work, or getting one of her uplifting text messages never failed to bring a smile to my face, and hope to my heart! Just as negativity breeds negativity, Hope breeds Hope, joy and peace!

7. Hope is like a candle that burns in the dark. I've heard it said that fear and faith can't live in the same space, and I believe this is true. I've also heard it often quoted that only light can drive out darkness, and I also believe this to be true. As I think about the darkness that accompanies fear, it is clear to me that faith and Hope are the light that will drive away the darkness of fear in our lives, and allow us to operate from a place of courage.

8. Hope leaves a legacy...of Hope! As I think about what I want to be known for in my life, it is clear to me that leaving a legacy of Hope, joy and peace is high on the list. I remember feeling very sad the day I received the news that Lynda had gone Home. I also remember that the sadness was very quickly followed by a feeling of peace because I knew that Lynda's journey had changed me for the good. My memories of Lynda will forever be memories of someone who lived her days with joy, peace and Hope. She inspired me every day to be the best version of me, and to not waste time on things that really don't matter!

9. Hope is powerful! What sustains a family through a tragedy, or a loss of a loved one, taken too soon (in our minds)? Only Hope. Without Hope, we perish; we live mired down in the pain of the past, in our regrets and sorrows. The power of Hope is astounding! Broken hearts can mend, lives can continue, there can be a future that is not filled with pain and regret. That is the power of Hope!

10. Hope is a decision that is made daily! I know that there were days through Lynda's journey where she was tired, and she probably had moments of doubt or fear that crept in. I know she had concerns about her family, and how they would live after her passing. And in the face of those daily concerns, she

had a daily decision to make...and so do we. Will we let the pain and fear of a broken and fallen world consume us, or will we step into Hope and live there in the fullness of God's promises?

Jesus promised that we would have difficulty, and let's be honest... the world can be a scary place! The beauty of the good news of Jesus is that we don't have to face that scary world alone, and with the Hope found in a solid faith and trust in Jesus, we can face the scary world with a brave and Hopeful heart!

Just like Lynda.

ABOUT KAREN WHITE

Karen White is a John Maxwell Certified Coach, Teacher and Speaker. As a *"DREAM Locksmith"* she helps people discover or rediscover their God-given dream, and become their *"best self."*

Helping others discover their gifts and talents and create a life where people life into their purpose is Karen's passion! Holocaust survivor Elie Wiesel once noted that at the end of our lives we won't be asked why we didn't accomplish certain things, but we will have to answer the question: *"Why didn't you become you? Why didn't you become all that you are?"* Karen wants to help others respond to that question with a resounding, *"I DID!"*

Karen has served with the US Air Force as both an active duty officer and civil service attorney for nearly 30 years. She began writing in 2015 because she aims to live by George Eliot's quote, *"It's never too late to be what you might have been!"*

Contact Karen:
- Website: www.JohnMaxwellGroup.com/KarenWhite
- Email: KarenWhite717@gmail.com
- Phone: 850-276-4504

OVERCOME FEAR BY EXERCISING COURAGE
By Terry Wood

OVERCOME FEAR BY EXERCISING COURAGE

It can be quite a daunting task to relay how we have learned to overcome FEAR by exercising COURAGE. We cannot think of COURAGE without considering FEAR as its antithesis. In order to better understand courage and fear, it may be helpful to reflect on these terms for a moment.

Fear can be understood from one of two different vantage points. It can be an opportunity to *"face everything and rise"* or *"face everything and run"*. Some of the greatest challenges in life depend on the focus of our fears.

Focus to remain resolute and determined can often be the difference between being victimized or victorious. It is in the common routine of life and the development of regular disciplines that will determine the *"rise"* or *"run"* concept, much like the fight or flight scenarios that often befall us in any given decision-making process. There are times when situations call for immediate response and a reaction takes place out of nowhere, we often call *"instinctive behavior"*. We are faced with a given circumstance and, without any hesitation or forethought, we react. Later, upon reflection, we find it was courage being exercised in faith and trust.

If we base our identity and focus on worldly measures such as an occupation, a relationship or perhaps even a desired status, it will only be a matter of time before disappointment and despair set in. All of those measures are fleeting, in that, they can be here one moment and gone the next.

For me, the beauty of courage is to recognize it is intrinsically *"tied to my mindset and developed over time, as I grow in faith."* This is where my courage is fortified, developed and strengthened. Therefore, it is important to realize that the exercise of growing in courage is the outflow of a trained mind, a seasoned heart and a confidence in our own personal identity.

Let me ask four helpful questions.

First, what is the origin of your fears? Fears are normally fed from the wellsprings of negative input, self-doubt and belief in lies.

One common definition for fear is *"False evidence appearing real"*. For some, fears are developed through unfulfilled expectations, relational disappointments, rejection or personal failures in the past. For others, fears often develop out of abusive behaviors, unhealthy controlling environments and traumatic experiences in the present. For many, fear becomes the common currency of navigation for tides of confusion and uncertainty of the future.

Second, when was the last time you recall being the recipient of unfulfilled expectations?

Third, can you remember the last time someone promised he would do something for you, only to have your expectations dashed or betrayed by him not following through with his word in action?

Fourth, when was the last time, perhaps, you were on the other side of the equation and failed to follow through with your word?

These are just a couple of ways expectations become shattered and cause us to become disillusioned and discouraged and often times embittered.

Courage is the virtue that allows us to overcome. Courage can be seen as the asset that facilitates genuine growth in godliness. Courage calls us to face the bold challenges of life with confidence and dependence. It is cloaked with humility and fortitude! To better illustrate this, use the following acronym when considering the true meaning of COURAGE.

Confidently
Overcoming
Urges of
Retreat
And
Guarded
Expectations

For some, courage can become a trite term that carries with it a sense of victory and achievement! For others, it can be a word that carries with it the full expression of experience for those who have overcome adversity, pain, failure and challenge. For too few, it is the action of exercising faith that culminates in accomplishment.

I liken courage to be the *"demonstration of faith that has acted on its prayers!"* A natural bi-product of courage is freedom. Freedom is obtained by walking in truth. However, before the truth can set us free, we must first realize what lie is holding us hostage. To better develop this concept of exercising courage by overcoming fear, consider heroes of faith like David, Moses and Joshua whose lives illustrate to us today how people grow in courage and overcome fear.

First, look at the life of David and his triumph over Goliath on behalf of the nation of Israel. Second, realize the disappointment of Moses who led his nation out of slavery, but never reached his destination due to his disobedience to the Lord. Third, examine the command of the Lord to Joshua to remain strong and courageous while leading the Israelites into the land of promise. Fourth, identify the true application of courage for believers as we examine the *"but God"* transitions from who we were before encountering Christ and who we are as a result of our transforming relationship with Christ.

How do we find the COURAGE that causes us to overcome fear? When will we realize how many God-given dreams you and I have left unfulfilled because fear placed us in a prison we could not escape? How many God-accomplishments with our names written on them have come, yet gone unaccomplished because fear paralyzed us? Are you tired of living in fear?

When we continue to choose to live in fear, our family, our friends, our church, our world misses out on our unique contribution. I will in essence rob God of His glory when I succumb to living in fear. As for me, I choose to no longer be classified as a glory thief of God!

As a man, it is still common for me to feel like that new freshman on a high school campus who is challenged by its sheer magnitude and I cannot remember where my locker is, much less its combination. It is about time you and I admit that there are occasions when we realize that we are afraid and that we also admit our moment by moment need of God to accompany us on those occasions. Only then can He show up and shine through our momentary lapses into discouragement and fear. These are opportunities for us to know and understand that we need to surrender to His leading and direction.

As a former athlete, from many years gone past, I can still recall the moments that gripped me as I headed into a competition or race with butterflies in my stomach only to subside once the opportunity to perform presented itself and the gun went off. The thrill of overcoming such fear subsided as adrenaline took over and I could rely on my routine of daily practice and discipline to get me through the next few moments that lie ahead.

In my everyday work world, it is not uncommon to be gripped by fear when I am presented with an unexpected challenge on a remodeling project or a large-scale job that should take several months to accomplish.

Fear is as common as breathing for some of us, but how we react to any given circumstance reveals our dependence on God and our need to not focus on the daunting task at hand. It is during these times I often refer to my *"How do you eat an elephant?"* mentality—by taking one bite at a time, by beginning the process of progress, much like starting a race and settling in on pace.

Two insights are easily derived from the story of David and Goliath (1 Samuel 17) on how to find courage in conquering our fears.

First, we must love God's glory more than our fears. We must be willing to surrender the emotions of fear that grip us from time to time in order to witness God working in and through our circumstances. David valued God's glory more than he valued his own life.

Second, we must ignore the criticism of cowards. Look at David, when selected to represent Israel in the battle with Goliath, his own brothers criticized him even though he was the only one who had enough faith in the power of his Creator to cause him to be able to stand before his enemy.

At the time when life presses in on us with daunting circumstances, most cowards will verbally attack us because we are willing to be courageous to do the things they only wished they had the courage to do. It is in times like these that true courage separates the men from the boys and allows us to rest in full confidence that remaining faithful in pressing times only grows our faith and deepens our walk in courage. These times allow us to create powerful outcomes while others focus on criticizing our efforts to remain steadfast and vigilant in the face of potential harm, perhaps even imminent death.

In short, these are some valuable lessons we can learn from the life of David as he was selected by God through King Saul to face Goliath in battle. David's confidence and courage should compel us to deepened trust, an unbridled love of God and victorious triumph!

If God could raise His son from the dead, can He not allow us to overcome our fear of rejection and ridicule? Moreover, it is almost natural for fear to grip us in our everyday living, but that fear need not paralyze us rendering us defeated.

What are those things that paralyze you more than giving God the glory that only He deserves by allowing us to find courage to stand in difficult times?

Is it a broken marriage, divorce, a hurting person? All of these things can be used to allow others to see and understand we are human and we are in need of a Savior that longs to touch hurting people. Fear can become our friend when and only when it pushes us into the presence of our Heavenly Father. Perhaps it's an addiction, or maybe you find yourself just cruising through life without a true sense of purpose and not able to reach your full redemptive potential because you and I are susceptible to the fear of failure.

It is only in the providence of God that when His children fail, we fail forward! It's ok to fail when a Sovereign God is our Father and we can trust Him to see us through them. As the saying of old goes, *"Better to have tried and failed than to have never tried and succeeded!"*

As a believer, I must trust that when I fail, I fail forward knowing that God has not promised me a life without failure, but rather He will be with me through it all. I must seek to allow Him to sustain me in my challenging times and place the glory in the end into His hands and not my circumstances.

Finally, it is necessary for me to be me and not try to be someone else in the throes of challenging times. Comparison with others becomes the great destroyer of courage and victory. If God wanted me to be somebody else, He would not have created me uniquely. He has created me with unique characteristics that separate me from every other person on the planet. He has divinely shaped me to fulfill His purposes in my life. Those purposes cannot be achieved by anyone else but me. He has called me to diligence, faithfulness, integrity, honesty and to ultimate victory! My identity is rooted in Christ and not determined by what I do, but rather it is rooted in what He has done. This is where I find great confidence to press on in challenging times and allow God to work in me, both to will and to do, according to His good pleasure.

Friend, know today that you have what it takes to stand in the face of trying circumstances, perhaps even danger and know that your Heavenly Father accompanies you in those overwhelming times! Surrender the fear of failure and rejection and walk in true peace and confidence and assured victory!

ABOUT TERRY WOOD

Terry is a husband, father, son, brother, friend and most importantly a Man Following Christ. His life passion is to reproduce reproducers for the Kingdom. He serves as a life coach, speaker, author, businessman and entrepreneur.

His pursuit of reproduction has been built on the intentional principles gained from 30 years of self-employment as a contractor and being immersed in College and Young Adult ministry for 26+ years as a layperson. He currently serves as a team leader in an Adult Bible Fellowship at his church. His passion is to see lives transformed through the application of biblical principles in marketplace environments and daily living.

Terry is a family man devoted to creatively releasing the reproduction of healthy life disciplines, which will develop servant leaders who fully engage the Lord as ambassadors, through acts of love and devotion to God and others. He resides in northern Indiana where he is active in raising his two sons, Zachary 13, and Jacob 9, along side of his wife Becky of 17 years. His involvement in local men's ministry provides opportunities to hire and mentor young men while teaching them a trade to become self-sufficient entrepreneurs.

He established Break the Yoke Ministries to come along side of men needing direction and input to break the cycle of addictive lifestyle behaviors patterns and/or incarceration. His business allows him to assist others toward personal freedom and balance in life.

Contact Terry:
- Facebook: www.Facebook.com/Battle-Ready-Warrior-552634461573562
- Email: BattleReadyWarrior@gmail.com

www.ingramcontent.com/pod-product-compliance
Lightning Source LLC
LaVergne TN
LVHW051244080426
835513LV00016B/1732